# CHASING WAVES

A Journey to Become the Best Captain on Fresh Water

## PAT WINTON

*Chasing Waves*
Second Edition

Copyright ©2025 Pat Winton Books
www.PatWinton.com

All rights reserved.
Thank you for buying an authorized edition of this book, and
for complying with copyright laws by not reproducing, scanning,
or distributing any part of it in any form without permission.
You are supporting writers and allowing us to share our stories.

Nautical tales of one couple's adventures while exploring the
Great Lakes and America's inland waterways and oceans.

*Design: Somberg Design, Ann Arbor, Michigan*
*Publishing resources: Postal Print, Dexter, Michigan*

ISBN/SKU: 9798989948437
ISBN: 979-8-9899484-3-7

# Thank You

### CYNTHIA FURLONG REYNOLDS
Cindy, leader of the Cedars Chips Writing Group, author of numerous books, short stories and newspaper articles, inspired me to begin writing. Under her enthusiastic leadership and encouragement, I have now completed my second book.
Thank You!

### MARTY SOMBERG
Marty, a talented and super graphic designer, inspired me to come out of my comfort zone and prepare the book in color. His graphic design of navigation charts is particularly spectacular.
Thank You!

### CEDARS WRITING GROUP
The members of the group were so patient and helpful as they listened and read my chapters. Their literary input, sometimes challenging, was very important to me. I want to particularly acknowledge JACKIE STICKNEY, who suggested *CHASING WAVES* as the title for the book. A Personal Thank You to each member!

### JORDON STYRK
Owner of PostalPlusPrints, Jordon provided the skill to scan prints and prepare files for the book. He also led me to make the book a 11 x 8 ½ design.
Thank You!

### CYNTHIA PINE
Cindy took the photos of me and the yacht backgrounds for the book.
Thank You!

*CHASING WAVES* — the book and adventures — wouldn't have been possible without the many colleagues, friends, fellow boaters, and waterways.

*The lure of the Great Lakes never ends.*

# Contents

CHAPTER 1   The Mystique of Lake Superior: Early Adventures   **7**

CHAPTER 2   Fresh-Water Island Living   **13**

CHAPTER 3   Preparing for Boating on The Great Lakes   **23**

CHAPTER 4   Lake Erie: Lake-of-the-Cat   **27**

CHAPTER 5   Lake Huron: "The Freshwater Sea"   **41**

CHAPTER 6   Lake Superior: Big Sea Waters   **59**

CHAPTER 7   Lake Michigan Summers   **79**

CHAPTER 8   Exploring the Welland Canal, Lake Ontario, and St. Lawrence River   **85**

CHAPTER 9   Our New Careers: Delivery Captain & First Mate   **95**

CHAPTER 10   Our Disastrous Great Loop Voyage   **99**

CHAPTER 11   Nine Days to Alaska   **107**

CHAPTER 12   My Career as a Delivery Captain, with Elaine as First Mate   **123**

CHAPTER 13   The Calamitous New Jersey Delivery   **127**

CHAPTER 14   Sea Ray Super Sport Challenge   **135**

CHAPTER 15   Managing Mud, Misery, and Rising Waters on a Luxury Meridian   **143**

CHAPTER 16   Pleasure and Perils During Group Getaways   **159**

I spent my early years living close to one large body of water—the Gulf of Mexico—but by the time I was seven, I was introduced to Lake Superior and discovered my fascination for Big Water.

# CHAPTER 1
# The Mystique of Lake Superior: Early Adventures

**WATER—BIG WATER**—has always been part of my life.

I entered into this world in St. Louis, Missouri, in 1939, when my father and mother, native Michiganders from the Upper Peninsula, were on their way from Upper Michigan to Houston, Texas. Our life on the south side of Houston, near Trinity and Galveston bays, was joyous and filled with interesting and exciting moments, even with the war raging.

The war required darkened windows, Dad serving as an air raid warden, margarine in bags with color packets to simulate butter, and the 1943 Surprise Hurricane that made landfall only a few miles from where we lived. At four years old, I remember the water blowing through our closed windows while I hid under my parents' bed.

A German submarine had just blown up one of our ammunition ships being loaded in Galveston Bay, and our shipbuilding neighbors lost co-workers in the explosion. My first memory with death. I remember early fears as we dealt with war-time separations and dangers for friends and neighbors.

I recall standing on the corner of our side street, saluting as I watched the extremely long convoys of solders and their equipment on their way to Galveston Harbor, to be loaded on ships destined for the war. Although I don't recall precisely, I believe the returning conveys were shorter.

We lived close to the Gulf of Mexico, and my early memories of big waters and adventures in Texas are rooted in day trips to Galveston to splash in the salt water, play in the gulf, and search for intriguing items on the beach, under Mother's watchful eye. Then those huge waves crashed into the sand castles I had worked so hard to build — they disappeared by the force of one wave.

Other memories include the Gene Autry Rodeo and Dad's Saturday paydays, when I rolled dice in the machinery shed with Dad's swamper, who believed I gave him good luck. (He was the man on the ground directing what was Dad's next move with his huge bulldozer.)

## GITCHE GUMEE

In early 1944, we moved to Ontonagon, Michigan, to live on the shores of Lake Superior in the Upper Peninsula. We were returning to Mother's home county and near Dad's childhood home in Iron County. The move was necessary due to my father's health challenges.

In the summer of 1946, at the age seven, I was baptized into the Big Sea Lady—my name for Lake Superior. She grasped my attention and has never let go.

Our introduction took place on the shore of the Shining Big Sea Water featured in Henry Wadsworth Longfellow's epic poem "The Song of Hiawatha." That day, the Big Sea Lady, also known as Gitche Gumee, took ahold of me, held me in her lap, then released me, after demonstrating her power. She gave me the first of many life lessons.

On that warm and sunny summer day, my father, mother, three-year-old sister, and I jumped into our 1936 Chevy Coupe, me in the rumble seat, and drove the several miles to the Ontonagon City Park on the shore of Lake Superior. A westerly breeze kept the black flies at bay, and the waves were merely small swells breaking just as they approached the beautiful sand beach. I couldn't wait to plunge into the lake. As I raced to the water, my father hollered, "Pat, be careful! There's a steep drop-off a short way off shore."

I found a good-sized log and slid it off the sand into the water. Straddling the log, I pretended to ride a horse as we glided over the small swells near the shoreline. Suddenly a wave reared its head out of nowhere, pulling us farther from shore. I don't recall crying out, but I do recall being terrified as I tried to bend over to paddle with my hand. Abruptly, my horse rolled, and I was dumped under water. I remember looking up and seeing the log far above me.

And then suddenly everything went dark.

I never did find out how my father rescued me, since he didn't swim. But somehow he rushed into the lake and was able to see me in the clear water. He grabbed me and pulled me out of the arms of the Big Sea Lady. I came to lying on my stomach, as he was pounding on my back to force water out of my lungs. I was choking as I sat up, but I was alive. I remember looking at the water and thinking, "I'm not afraid of you."

"We are so very lucky you didn't drown!" Mother gasped.

## LAKE SUPERIOR

North America's five Great Lakes were most likely formed during the Ice Age. Lake Superior, the grand Big Sea Lady, is the largest of the five and has the world's largest freshwater surface area, as well as the world's third-largest volume of fresh water: ten percent of the entire world's fresh water. Her water is COLD all year, averaging thirty-four degrees. As a result, She is known for keeping Her dead. You see, Her low temperatures don't permit bacteria to form in drowned victims, so the body decay is so reduced that the body cannot rise to the surface.

Lake Superior is also the deepest of the five Great Lakes, at 1,333 feet. Her long west-to-east location, depth, and the prevailing winds from the west and northwest combine to cause waves to enlarge to alarming heights in a short time. During the tragic November storm that sank the *Edmund Fitzgerald* in 1975, it is said that three gigantic forty-foot waves moved along most of Her 350-mile length, leaving devastation in their wake.

Experts have written that when a drop of water leaves the lake via the St. Marys River, (a twenty-five-foot drop of rapids, and the only outlet), its journey takes approximately two hundred years to cross Lake Huron, Lake Erie, Lake Ontario, and the St. Lawrence River before reaching the Atlantic Ocean. In addition, environmentalists suggest that draining Lake Superior would take about two hundred years, presuming no water was entering from the land watershed, which includes countless lakes and rivers. Therefore, I theorize that some of the water I swallowed and expelled before my father rescued me has not yet reached the Atlantic Ocean.

## AN ANGRY BIG SEA LADY

After my father died in 1946, my mother, sister, and I moved to the southern part of Ontonagon County, about thirty miles from Lake Superior, which meant I had few opportunities to swim on Her. I missed Her cold water— just kidding—but I really did miss seeing the magnitude and power of Her waves crashing onto the shoreline, particularly in the October and November storms.

In the summer of 1948, when I was nine, I was invited to return to Lake Superior when Uncle Martin Kallio and my cousins came to visit from Detroit. The weather was perfect for lake trout fishing, and my uncle asked my local two cousins and me if we wanted to join them for a chartered fishing trip. I remember how excited I was, as I had never even dreamed of riding in a boat on the Big Sea Lady.

A date was set. Uncle Martin collected those of us from Trout Creek, and we headed to Ontonagon very early on the day of the charter. What an exhilarating experience to be out on the lake! Her surface was flat and shining as we headed from Ontonagon's

# "As we tried to race for home, each new wave seemed to be much higher than the last as the storm caught up with us."

harbor toward the lake trout area west of the Porcupine Mountains, approximately twenty miles from Ontonagon.

To this day, I've seldom experienced such an impressive fishing haul. We caught so many lake trout that they filled an old-time wash tub. What a fantastic time we had!

The following summer, I was thrilled to hear that Uncle Martin and my cousins were coming again to go charter fishing. Again, I was invited. I counted the days, and they crawled by. This time, however, our experience would be very different.

I had observed the fury of Gitchee Gumee when we lived in Ontonagon, and later I had walked the breakwall when She was angry, but I was about to witness first-hand Her anger—and I'll never forget that day.

Six of us climbed aboard a smaller boat with a different captain on a beautiful summer morning. The captain set a course toward the Porcupine Mountains, like we did the year before. After twenty miles or more on the open water, we all followed the captain's orders and set up the trolling gear. Each one of us had our own assignments. Unfortunately, to our disappointment, we weren't catching the quantities of lake trout we had caught the prior year. This captain's system was different. I was only ten, but I thought we were trolling in a different area of the Big Sea Lady. We were much farther from shore.

The west wind began to pick up after about an hour, and clouds were quickly forming on the western horizon. I had been assigned a forward fishing position on the port side. As a result, I occasionally looked to the west when we were trolling in that direction. Gazing up at the western sky, I suddenly saw a very strange sight, and I shouted to the captain, "Look out to the west! I can't see the water. Everything looks green!"

The captain took one look and shouted, "All lines in NOW! Put on your life jackets!"

He proceeded to assist us as we pulled in our lines. We were delayed getting underway because some of our lines had crossed and the captain had to sort them out. After what seemed like a very long time, we were finally underway, heading back to Ontonagon on what normally should have been a two-hour trip. Everyone occasionally glanced back at the advancing storm.

The wind was steadily increasing, and so were the waves. The captain maintained the boat's maximum speed, but he began fighting waves that were towering over us. As the wooden lap-streaked boat with its center console and single-screw inboard engine cut into the next wave, we were driven to the top, and then the bow dropped very quickly into the trough before we climbed up the next wave. I did notice the captain watching to see if the wave behind us was catching up to us—which meant it could sink our boat. Moving along with the waves in this fashion is called "motoring in a following sea." It is a very exciting way to travel—but very unnerving.

As we tried to race for home, each new wave seemed to be much higher than the last as the storm caught up with us. The waves, now more than six feet high, began to create another problem. When the bow dropped off the top, the propeller would occasionally come out of the water, causing the engine to rev to a high rpm before the propeller re-entered the water. In later years, I learned what I suspected as a

# "Three times when I was a boy, Gitchee Gumee took me and held me in Her mighty watery arms."

boy: this is a very dangerous condition, since the high-rpm propeller can break off a blade when it is suddenly driven down into the water. I clung to the center console handrail with all my strength and let my body move with the boat's movement.

The captain began trying to quarter the waves to keep the prop in the water, but this caused the boat to veer off the shortest course to the safety of Ontonagon Harbor. Quartering a wave means the boat goes up the wave at roughly a 45-degree angle, and after going over the top and starting down the backside of the wave, the boat is turned back, so it once again climbs up the next wave at an angle. The net effect is the boat has to travel much farther to get to a distant point—in this case, the safety of Ontonagon Harbor. The thrashing Big Sea Lady was having Her way with us, and a couple of cousins were becoming very pale. I'm sure everyone was as terrified as I was.

As we finally approached the Ontonagon River entrance, the storm was raging directly on top of us, with waves eight feet or more. The entrance breakwater rock wall was at an angle to us. The incoming giant waves slamming into the wall threw the water more than fifteen feet in the air. I remember thinking, "How are we going to enter at this angle? We should be coming directly into the opening!"

"Get down on the floor and hang on to each other! NOW!" the captain shouted.

I don't know why, but I continued to stand next to the captain while I was hanging onto the waist-high bar that was adjacent to the center helm. Frozen in shock at the terrifying sight, I was certain we were going to crash into the end of the breakwater. It was then I heard the captain say in a quiet voice, "I've got one shot. I can't turn around!"

At the moment the boat dropped to the bottom of the wave we had been riding, he abruptly threw the throttle forward for full power. The boat leapt forward and slipped past the outside end of the south breakwater. We were literally shot into the calm water of the entrance.

We were safe!

Even though we all knew how close our fishing trip had come to a disaster, everyone cheered, thrilled to be safely home. Later, the captain thanked me for calling out what I had seen on the horizon, so he had time—but barely— to return to port.

I knew the Big Sea Lady had decided to give us another day, but I also believe that on the dramatic dash for port, She wanted me to know Her fury and capability. And She was rewarding us for the captain's skilled handling of a small boat, knowing that She could easily have smashed the boat and its passengers to pieces.

I should also mention that Uncle Martin and cousins never again asked if we wanted to go charter fishing on Lake Superior.

Thanks to a highly skilled captain, I learned an invaluable lesson about the way talented and veteran captains could outwit Her. I have never forgotten that captain's maneuver. It has helped me on a number of occasions during my more than twenty years as a captain on the Great Lakes.

But the Big Sea Lady had more to teach me.

### BIG SEA LADY'S OFF-SHORE WIND

In 1957, when I was eighteen and preparing to leave Michigan's Upper Peninsula for college, my friend Bill asked if my girlfriend Vera and I wanted to go for a evening canoe ride on Lake Superior. He needed a canoeing partner and explained that it would be fun to drop the canoe in at the Floodwood River and canoe the one mile along the Superior shoreline to the Cranberry River.

On this beautiful late-August evening, the Big Sea Lady appeared very calm when we departed around eight o'clock. In fact, She was so calm that we hardly saw a ripple on the water. Bill took the position in the stern, mainly for steering and paddling, and I took the bow position for power paddling. Vera sat on a cushion in the center.

As we leisurely made our way along the glassy surface, a very strong off-shore wind fiercely kicked up and caught us by surprise—at a time when, unfortunately, we had been lured farther from shore.

Suddenly, the Big Sea Lady had us in her grip, and She wasn't about to let go. We quickly turned and tried to paddle to the shore, but we couldn't overcome the wind, which was threatening to blow us out into the abyss of Lake Superior.

She was playing with our canoe as if it were a toy. When we tried to move at an angle to the shore, Her wind would actually blow the bow so it was pointing outward, farther away from shore.

Without discussing the matter, Bill and I both knew our only hope was to keep the bow pointing into the wind, which continued to increase in strength. As it blew harder and harder, we paddled harder and harder.

We repeatedly dug our paddles deep into the water, but no matter how hard we worked, we were unable to move closer to shore. Vera moved to one side of the canoe and used her hand and arm as an auxiliary paddle. At some point, we realized that we didn't have life jackets—not a good feeling. No one was talking. Fear filled the canoe. Bill asked, "Did anyone tell someone what we were going to do?"

Silence!

We tried every maneuver we could think of. Paddle fast. Paddle deep and hard. Take long strokes. But whenever we thought we might be making headway, a strong gust pushed us farther from shore.

By the time the sun was fast sinking into what appeared to be the Big Sea Lady, we had been paddling for hours. My strength was leaving me, fear was overwhelming me, and I was almost ready to give up. And then I wondered if the wind might be dying.

We all paused, as we glanced quickly at each other, sharing the same thought. But sure enough, when we resumed paddling with our fiercely aching arms and our entire bodies hurting, the wind began to change to the west. At this point, the sun was almost out of sight beyond the Big Sea Lady.

She was loosening Her grip as the sun set!

We shot a glance at the shore and determined we were actually moving closer. With renewed strength, breathing very hard, we paddled as if our lives depended on it—and they did. We kept expecting another gust to blow, but it didn't come.

The three of us finally reached shore after dark, totally exhausted after nearly three hours of extreme exertion. We stumbled out of the canoe and collapsed on the sand. I devoutly thanked the Lord that She had finally let us go.

Three times when I was a boy, Gitchee Gumee took me and held me in Her mighty watery arms. In Her way, She cleansed me with a cold-water baptism, then She released her grip on me, so I could live and return another day.

These early experiences on the Gulf of Mexico and Lake Superior instilled my love and desire to be on the water. But whenever I am on or near the Big Lady, I have strange and conflicting feelings that are difficult to explain. I believe they are deep feelings of respect, definitely laced with fear. ■

*Our island living began with a dream and an architectural plan drawn by a friend.*

# CHAPTER 2
# Fresh-water Island Living

**I WAS FORTUNATE** to meet Elaine Marie Killey on a blind date after my first year at General Motors Institute (now Kettering University). This fantastic woman stole my heart the first time we met. Wow, what an awesome gal.

Months after we began dating, I asked if she wanted to visit Lake Superior, meet my family in Ontonagon County, eat Finnish nissua and pasties, and perhaps take a true Finnish sauna. I explained that she would have to ride a Greyhound bus from Flint to Watersmeet and endure a fourteen-hour, six-hundred-mile ride with multiple stops and possibly two bus changes. Without any hesitation, she said, "Yes."

I had fallen in love with a woman who, like me, wasn't afraid of new experiences and challenges.

When she arrived in Ontonagon County, one of our visits was to Ontonagon and Lake Superior. As we walked the sand beach, I told her of my near-drowning experience when I was seven, and how I felt when I was near the Big Sea Lady.

She recalled how she loved to spend time on Lake Huron, how she enjoyed the sand beach and swimming, since her family lived only a block from the beach. As she took off her shoes and waded into Lake Superior, she screamed, "It's so cold! How could you swim in this?"

We were married in June 1961, and our adventurous life journey began immediately.

In time, we had two sons, and Elaine and I enjoyed visiting her parents' cottage with the boys. Brian and Craig grew up swimming, riding in Grandpa's ski boat, and fishing from his old metal rowboat. Elaine and I talked about one day owning lakeside waterfront property, so we could be on the water on weekends and during vacations in the summer. We might even have a cottage that would accommodate family and friends who didn't have opportunities to enjoy time on the water.

In 1966, five years after our marriage, we were visiting Elaine's family cottage on Sage Lake in Ogemaw County, when our on-the-water dream began to materialize. Four-year-old Brian and one-year-old Craig were basking in the sunshine as we took a slow afternoon boat ride with Elaine's parents, studying the shore lined with cottages and a few vacant lots. As we rode around Middle Island, one of the three islands on Sage Lake, we saw a recently posted sign on the island: LOT FOR SALE, followed by a phone number.

Elaine's father immediately turned the boat toward the island. As soon as we reached the sandy beach, Elaine and I jumped out onto the sand and began walking the island lot, which faced westward on the kidney-shaped island's narrow center. The terrain was elevated at the back of the lot, making it a perfect place to build. It was easy to assume the rear lot wasn't large enough for a cottage because the water line is only a short distance from the island's centerline. "Maybe we could buy the back lot later and own all the land across the island," I commented as we returned to the front lot.

When we faced the lake from the spot where a cottage would most likely be built, our westward view of the sunset was unobstructed and breathtaking.

"Imagine what the sunsets will look like," Elaine murmured. "Just think how wonderful to live on an island we could only reach by boat. What an adventure!"

*Two tired girls relax after swimming all day.*

"Hon, I think this is the answer to our prayers," I responded as we climbed back into the boat. "Does anyone have a pencil and paper, so we can write down the phone number?"

### MIDDLE ISLAND ON SAGE LAKE

On the Monday following our exploration of Middle Island, I called the property owner to learn more about the island as soon as I could take a break at work. He said the lot we wanted could be purchased on a land contract for $1,200. The Middle Island Home Owners Association owned property and water frontage on the mainland, to provide individual dockage and car parking for the thirty-two lots, and the association also had the rights to use a barge for moving supplies to the island.

When I reported this news, Elaine immediately insisted, "Let's buy it!"

I was a little more cautious—but not much. "We also need to buy our first boat to go to and return from our island. Then we'll be islanders!"

As soon as we finalized the purchase, the planning and preparations began. We were now islanders preparing for a life on the water.

Fortunately for us, my work colleague had decided to change careers and become an architect. One morning on our commute to work, he told me he was attending night school. His program required him to design a stand-alone building and have it approved for construction. He asked if he could design our cottage.

Without any hesitation, I agreed. Our vacation home journey began that day.

After preliminary sketches and discussions, we agreed on a modified A-frame cottage with a kitchen, downstairs bedroom, bathroom, living room, and most importantly, Elaine's loft for the children. Elaine envisioned a large dining table right in front of the large west-facing picture window. A sliding glass back door provided a view of sunrises reflecting off the lake on the back side of the island.

### BUILDING THE ISLAND HOME

Elaine and I used the winter of 1967-68 to prepare and make detailed plans for what had to be done in the summer. At the top of the list was purchasing a boat. Even before the lake ice melted, Elaine located a used, fourteen-foot fiberglass boat with a fifty-horsepower Mercury outboard and a trailer.

On a cold, dreary April day in 1968, we drove to Sage Lake from Royal Oak, pulling our first boat and trailer with two excited young boys along for the adventure. With our new boat in the water, life jackets on, everyone taking in the moment, we cruised the one mile to the island to discover the cement blocks, sand, and gravel piled and ready to be used to build the foundation and hook up our sewer system. Another sign that the Lord was watching over this project.

We finished the cottage in the summer of 1969. Thus began our life on the waters of Sage Lake. Her waters provided day and night transportation, swimming, fishing, water skiing, and sailing. The lake challenged us with thick fog, storms, a visible tornado on the lake, beautiful yet frightening lightning, rolling thunder, and rolling waves as we traveled to and from the mainland. Over the years, her beautiful sun and moon reflections continued to live in our memories. Our love of life on the water was nurtured and grew on Sage Lake.

Elaine took the responsibility of operating the boat, and she learned to maneuver it with great skill. In those days we didn't have cell phones or even a phone on the island, so whenever a hardware store or grocery store run was needed, Elaine was the captain and shopper. At times she was the captain during thunderstorms, with lightning all around, and there were nights when she left the island in thick fog to return guests to the mainland.

The boys rode wake boards as early as six or seven and quickly advanced to water skis. Elaine was their excellent captain, always operating a safe boat.

*Deanna first visited Sage Lake when she was ten weeks old, and she grew into a proud fisherwoman during our summers there.*

*Sage Lake, Ogemaw County*

*The distance between the landing and our dock is one mile.*

FRESH-WATER ISLAND LIVING

> "On a cold spring afternoon in April of 1972, we brought a very special first-time visitor to our island: our daughter Deanna, who was ten weeks old."

We wore out the original fifty-horsepower engine and replaced it with a new sixty-five-horsepower Mercury outboard. Later, we bought a used sixteen-foot Duo and installed our new Mercury motor on it. Within two years, we were operating our second boat.

## OUR FIRST BIG WATER ADVENTURE

From our relatively minor Sage Lake boating experiences, we began to explore larger waters. Friends whose parents owned a summer home on Bois Blanc Island, Lake Huron, invited us to spend a weekend with them. We immediately accepted.

I decided to trailer our boat to Cheboygan and use it on Lake Huron. The six-mile cruise would be challenging, but since the island and mainland were visible to each other, what could possibly happen?

At least this is what I told my family.

Our two-hour drive to Cheboygan was uneventful, and we launched our boat into the Cheboygan River. After passing down the river, we entered a calm and blue Lake Huron, with Bois Blanc Island plainly in sight in the distance. Our compass heading to the Bois Blanc Marina was perfect. As we entered into the island harbor breakwater, we saw Joel and his family there to greet us.

During our stay, we toured the island and heard the stories of Al Capone's time there as he recovered from wounds and hid from federal marshals. And more stories about the battles of the French, British, Americans, and indigenous peoples that had taken place in the late 1700s and early 1800s.

I had decided that we would depart early the morning of our last day, but when we arrived at the Bois Blanc Marina, we faced solid fog over Lake Huron. I wondered if the fog also covered the mainland.

But we were accustomed to fog on Sage Lake. Elaine and I had learned to navigate in very solid fog using a compass and keeping track of time to make the necessary turns. I knew the compass heading from Bois Blanc Marina to the Cheboygan River entrance, so I assured the family the fog wouldn't be a problem. "It's only six miles straight across, and we can hear the fog horn near the entrance to the river."

Joel begged us to stay and wait for the fog to lift, but I was certain all would be fine. We donned our life jackets, climbed into the boat, and entered the abyss. The lake was calm, which is common when the fog sits on the water, and we stayed on our heading. But when we heard sounds coming from the south and growing louder, I realized that something very large was moving toward us.

All of a sudden, through the thick fog we saw a huge ocean vessel coming in our direction. I didn't panic, since the giant was not coming directly at us. I slowed our boat almost to a stop to keep us out of its path.

The ocean vessel passed us at a very high speed. I panicked when I saw the six-to-eight-foot wake streaking across the water toward us. I later learned that these vessels produce a much larger wake than the Great Lakes freighters, due to their ocean hull design. The memory of being on the Big Sea Lady and surviving the storm on our fishing trip inspired me to react like the fishing boat captain.

*Our boys grew up on the lake, mastering water sports at early ages.*

# "This new life motivated us to return to the water in a new way, challenged by wind, waves, and weather."

Yelling to our sons to come forward and sit on the floor in front of Elaine, I threw the throttle forward and turned the boat to port (left), to attempt to outrun the wake moving at us. Our fifty-horsepower outboard moved the boat quickly, and I managed to keep us away from the wake. I knew it would eventually reduce in height.

I finally decided to quarter the wake, like the Lake Superior fishing boat captain had done. Our fifteen-foot boat rose up on the wake and safely slid down the back side. We bounced around a bit, but we were safe.

And then the next level of panic set in. I didn't know where we were. I had lost track of our heading and had no idea how long we had traveled.

What if another vessel was following this one?

As we sat dead in the water, still rocking in the boat from the after-effects of the large wake, I attempted to guess how far we had traveled in my panic maneuver. What should be the new compass heading?

"Listen for sounds like those we just heard," I told everyone while we sat quietly in the solid fog.

The panic subsided as I realized we were all safe. I made my best guess on a compass heading, and we slowly moved in that new direction. When Brian heard the distant fog horn, he immediately pointed in its direction, and we headed toward the sound. Suddenly we emerged into bright sunlight. The river entrance was right in front of us. Resting alongside the parking lot dock, we took a moment to breathe and silently thanked the Lord for our safety.

This was our first scary situation on the Great Lakes in our own vessel, but it certainly wasn't going to be the last. I had tasted the challenge of navigating a tiny boat on big water, and I began dreaming of becoming a captain on the Great Lakes.

## DEANNA'S FIRST VISIT TO MIDDLE ISLAND

On a cold spring afternoon in April of 1972, we brought a very special first-time visitor to our island: our daughter Deanna, who was ten weeks old. The air temperature was most likely in the low forties, since the ice had just melted and the winds were from the north.

Elaine carefully wrapped Deanna with extra blankets as she confessed she was afraid. "Pat, are you sure it will be safe to go to the cottage?"

After the boys and I reassured Elaine, we prepared the homemade life raft the boys and I had designed for the boat ride in case of a disaster. We took a flat life-saving cushion and tied life jackets around the perimeter to provide a small boat where Deanna could be laid if necessary. Elaine wanted to hold her, so we placed the life boat on the seat between Elaine and me. Not quite a reed basket like Moses had, but very substantial and safe. After we put on our life jackets and carefully placed Deanna into her mother's arms, we pushed off for the mile-long trip to our island home.

Everyone was nervous as we very slowly moved onto the lake. Sage Lake was very flat and calm, as if welcoming Deanna to her waters. All of us were silent on the trip, but we safely landed on the island and opened the cottage. Deanna, at ten weeks old, was initiated into island living and water voyages.

## COMMUTING TO WORK

When we lived in Beaverton, Elaine took the children to Sage Lake for the summer, and I commuted to work.

One foggy morning, I was about to depart from the cottage when out of the fog appeared a small boat with two fishermen trolling for bass along the deep drop-off in front of our cottage.

I suddenly had an idea. Wearing my business suit and carrying my briefcase, I grabbed my fishing pole and headed to our pontoon boat. The fishermen had already trolled around the end of the island when I was finally underway. I took a standing position at the helm while holding my briefcase and steering wheel with one hand and the fishing rod at an angle in the other, as if I had a line out and was trolling.

As I came through the fog and into sight of the other fishing boat, the men began pointing and laughing so hard I thought they would tip over. With both hands busy, I stood tall, smugly cruising by them. I laughed all the way to the office.

## MOVING ON

It was a sad and thankful day in 1989, when we sold the cottage. We had moved to Ohio in 1982, the boys were in college, and my job limited the time we could have on Sage Lake. God was at work again, as the sale of the cottage permitted me to purchase my company.

This new life motivated us to return to the water in a new way, challenged by wind, waves, and weather. This time our adventures would be on the waters of the Great Lakes, and eventually on the oceans off North America. I set a goal to become the best captain of pleasure craft on the big waters. ■

*This is how I always remember the beauty and tranquility of life on the water.*

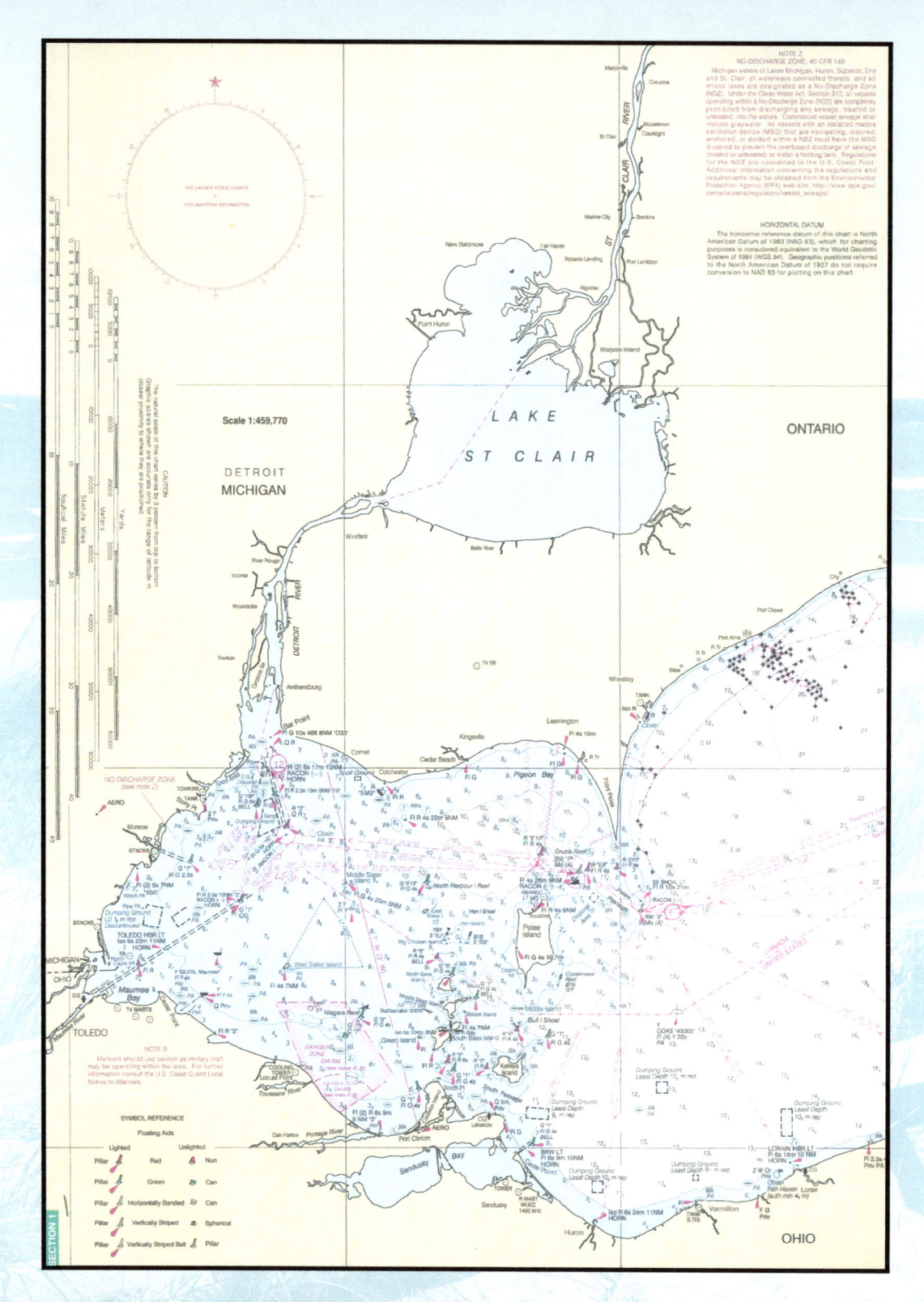

# CHAPTER 3
# Preparing for Boating on The Great Lakes

## OUR TRANSITION

OUR ISLAND LIVING on Sage Lake, begun in June 1969, offered the freedom and tranquility to watch a sunset and sunrise, as well as birds in flight while we aimlessly floated on the water. It restored our senses.

During those years, Elaine and I had a number of opportunities to sail on Lake St. Clair out of the Grosse Point Yacht Club. Those sun-filled summer afternoons inspired us to take a sailing course offered in Bay City, where we learned rules of the road, navigation, life-saving devices and procedures, federal and state regulations, and boat nomenclature.

New friends in the sailing class invited us to join them on their sailboat on Lake Huron's Saginaw Bay. One day while sailing on the bay, the wind died, and we took long hours to return to Bay City.

Despite our enjoyment of these adventures, we decided that my profession required a specific return time, and sailing was too unpredictable. Relying on the wind and/or a five-HP outboard to return to port wasn't going to work for us.

## OUR FIRST BOAT ON THE GREAT LAKES

After moving to Ohio, near Dayton, we found ourselves totally land-locked. We missed the water. In February of 1992, on the spur of a moment, I suggested, "Let's go to Lake Erie," and Elaine agreed.

It happened to be the February weekend when the 1992 Lake Erie Boat Show was held in Cleveland. We wandered into Catawba Island's Treasure Cove Sea Ray Dealership and Marina, admired the new 1992 Sea Rays on display, and met the dealership owners. They assured us that if we purchased a new boat, we could keep it in their marina and have all the amenities boating and living onboard at a single location could offer—and the drive there was only two-and-one-half hours from our home.

Our visit to Port Clinton and Catawba Island opened our eyes to a new and wonderful world with access to the waters of all the Great Lakes. All those old memories and adventures on Lake Superior returned. Maybe we could visit Her!

Elaine was very much in favor of the purchase, knowing we could motor out and back to the marina regardless of weather conditions. We made decisions quickly in the next few days. A 1992 Sea Ray 290 Sundancer with a single big block V-8 outdrive was ordered, with delivery scheduled for the opening of the marina at the end of April, 1992. Thus began our twenty-five-year adventure on the challenging and breathtakingly beautiful Great Lakes.

Our first challenge was to select a name for the vessel. Choosing a woman's name is a tradition that has existed since the beginning of boating. Because this was a very important decision, we struggled to come up with the perfect name.

*Treasure Cove Marina became our home-away-from-home in 1992.*

One day I commented to Elaine that I had two very significant women in my life: Elaine and Deanna. "ELEANA is the name I want for our new boat. ELE for Elaine and ANA for Deanna." I don't recall any objections, and the decision was made.

According to my understanding, boat names shouldn't be reused for another boat. Some people get around this tradition by using a I, II, and III, but we kept the identical name, ELEANA, for all four of our Great Lakes boats.

## INITIATION AT TREASURE COVE MARINA

Our dock assignment at Treasure Cove was at the far end of the marina, adjacent to its water entrance/exit. This was convenient for loading and unloading the car, but with only one other boat in the vicinity, winds from 360 degrees made docking a serious challenge.

I believe some of the seasoned boaters in the marina couldn't wait to see the Wintons enter the marina and watch the maneuvers I would make to get the boat close enough for Elaine to lasso a dock

*Elaine poses at Treasure Island with our brand new 290 Sea Ray, our first Great Lakes boat.*

piling and pull the boat into the dock. Our Middle Island dock had been protected from the winds, so docking there had been very easy to accomplish—and it was done without an audience of experienced boaters watching and laughing.

With persistence, I was determined to master this endeavor, and finally the ribbing subsided. I became proud of my skill at sliding the boat into the slip and stopping so that Elaine only had to reach out and drop the lines onto the boat cleats.

The boat traffic in and out of West Harbor Basin, the huge harbor where Treasure Cove Marina was located, was beyond belief. Two separate entrances from Lake Erie emptied into the narrow, north/south, two-mile-long harbor. Along the harbor's west shoreline sat our marina and eight additional marinas. In addition, many private trailer parks and homes used the harbor.

On July 4, 2010, the Coast Guard counted 10,000 boats in the West Erie Basin, probably three times the number you'll see there now. It didn't take very long to learn the accepted and most often used traffic patterns. But we also learned to recognize the boaters who didn't follow the rules of the road. Our dock location provided a broad view of traffic stops made by the sheriff and Coast Guard. Many times we encountered the boaters who thought, "The size of my boat determines the right of way."

This was the beginning of our twenty-five year journey on the fresh waters of American and Canadian Great Lakes and inland waters. ∎

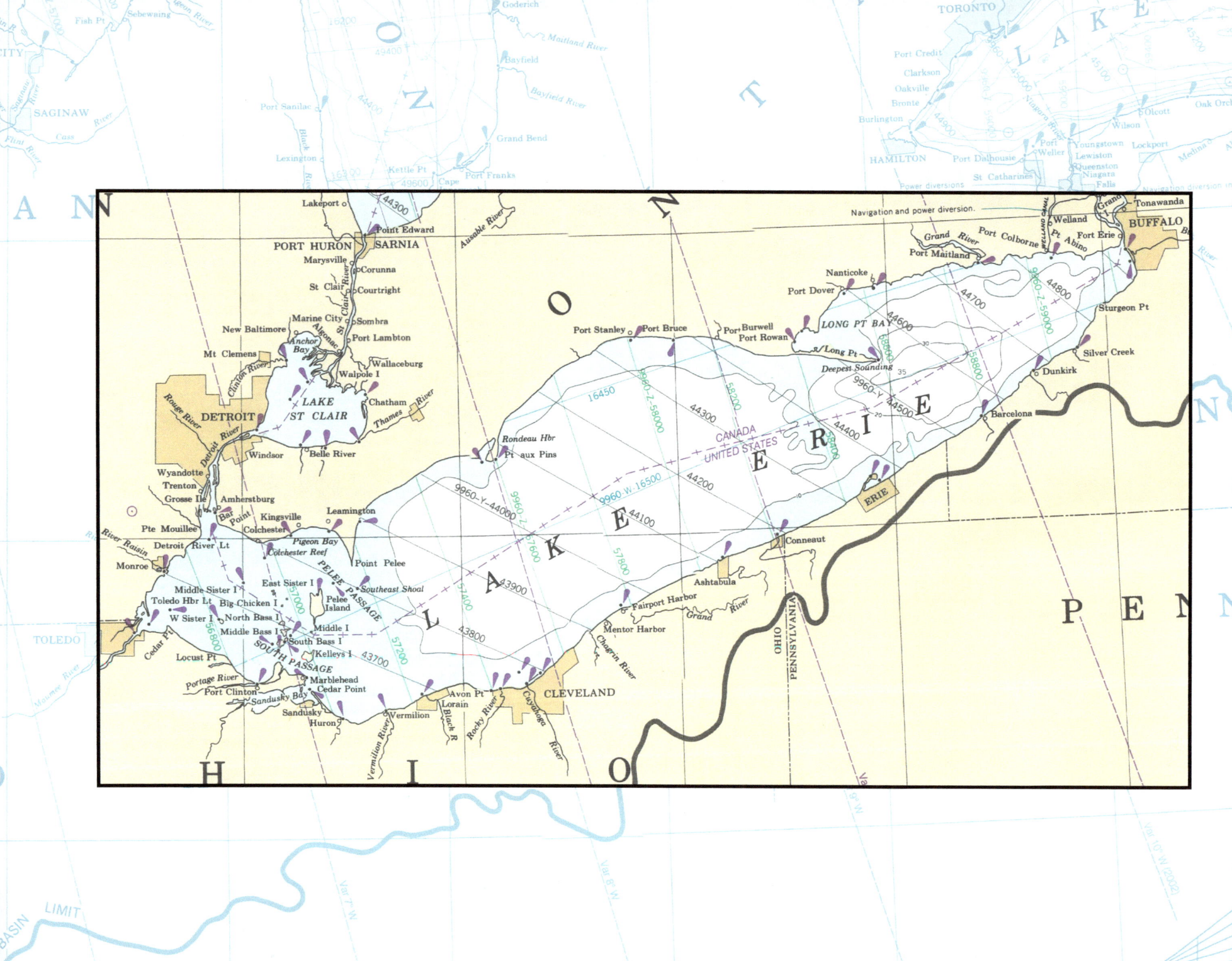

CHAPTER 4

# Lake Erie: Lake-of-the-Cat

**SPENDING OUR WEEKENDS** and vacations back on the water was exhilarating. What could possibly be better than living on a boat in the middle of the western basin of Lake Erie? We had daily opportunities to visit Put-in-Bay on South Bass Island, Cedar Point Amusement Park, Kelleys Island, and Port Clinton, all within ten miles of our dock. If weather didn't cooperate on the lake, there were many other activities, since the area is a Mecca of restaurants, sightseeing, and shopping.

We were suddenly thrust into a new world of boating terminology and new developments in boating navigation and capabilities. What we found most rewarding was making friends with like-minded boaters, meeting special characters, and becoming acquainted with families from all over the state and beyond. Another main attraction for me was learning how to catch Lake Erie's famous perch and walleye.

Wonderful weekends were filled with something new on every wave.

According to what I've read, the Lake Erie basin was carved out between one million and 12,600 years ago. Ancient lake outflow formed the river that created Niagara Falls, as well as the Niagara River. Water inflow from what is now Lake Huron contributed to the formation of Lake Erie. The lake as we know it is about 4,000 years old.

According to historians, the southern shore of Lake Erie was dominated by the Eriez Indians, who were also known as the "Cat People" because they wore robes of cougar, puma, and panther. The Dutch called them "Erielhonan," meaning "long-tails," or in French, "Lake-of-the-Cat." The Iroquois Indians told the French and Dutch explorers that the Eriez shot arrows soaked in rattlesnake venom during their wars. According to my research, they were the only North American tribe known to do this.

The French-Canadian explorer Louis Joliet is normally credited as the first white man to see Lake Erie, in 1669. Erie was the last of the Great Lakes to be discovered.

Early explorers traveled from Ottawa, now the capital of Canada, to the North Channel of Lake Huron's Georgian Bay, or to Lake Ontario and then to the southeastern end of Georgian Bay. Using these waterways, early explorers avoided the dangerous Eriez and Iroquois tribes on the south shore of Lake Erie.

Early New World settlers moving by land from the Northeast traveled south to St. Louis to enter into the Midwest territories. I theorize that the Eriez tribes and their reputation kept settlers from traveling along the southern shore of Lake Erie. Additionally, the Black Swamp, which extended along the south shore of Lake Erie from Sandusky Bay, Ohio, nearly all the way to Fort Wayne, Indiana, made passage almost impossible. When early settlers took the short cut through the mosquito-infested Black Swamp to reach the western frontier, many contracted malaria.

I consider Lake Erie to be two lakes in one. Overall, the lake is 241 miles in length and fifty-seven miles at its widest point. The western basin lies west of an imaginary line drawn southward from Ontario's Pelee Island and Ohio's Kelleys Island to the Ohio's north

*Kelleys Island is famous for its dramatic Glacial Grooves, which are four hundred feet long, thirty-five feet wide, and fifteen feet deep.*

shore. This west basin is approximately fifty miles in length and thirty-seven miles wide, with an average depth of only twenty-seven feet. In contrast, the eastern basin's depth varies from sixty feet to 211 feet at its deepest point. Because the lake basically lies in an east-to-west formation, it is subject to the prevailing westerly and northeasterly winds.

According to scientists, Lake Erie's water completely changes every 2.6 years, thereby helping to keep it relatively clean, despite the fact it is the collection point for all the pollutants and debris from Lake Superior, Lake Michigan, Lake Huron, the St. Clair River, Lake St. Clair, and the Detroit River.

Lake Erie's western basin holds eleven islands in the main body of water, with numerous reefs and small islands closer to shorelines.

The four main Canadian islands lie in the Province of Ontario. Pelee is the largest of all Erie islands and is inhabited. Middle Sister, East Sister, and Middle Island are uninhabited.

Erie's islands in the United States all rest in the state of Ohio. Five are inhabited: Kelleys, the largest; North Bass; Middle Bass; South Bass; and Rattlesnake. Green and West Sister are uninhabited.

These islands all have significant histories with indigenous people. Kelleys Island is most famous for its Glacial Grooves, which are four hundred feet long, thirty-five feet wide, and fifteen feet deep. More than sixty archaeological sites have been discovered on Kelleys Island alone, the most famous being Inscription Rock, with markings dating as far back as 12,000 years ago.

One of the largest naval battles of the War of 1812 was the Battle of Put-in Bay, which took place just west of South Bass Island. This is where Admiral Oliver Hazard Perry defeated the British on September 10, 1813, thereby earning a Congressional Gold Medal and the Thanks of Congress. Perry's leadership significantly accounted for the success of all nine of Lake Erie's military victories during that war with England. He is also remembered for the words on his battle flag: "Don't give up the ship." Words I strongly echo! He is also known for his message to General William Henry Harrison: "We have met the enemy, and they are ours."

The islands once were home to the Eastern Massasauga Rattlesnake, which is now, I believe, extinct on the islands. During our twenty-seven years on Catawba Island, we became acquainted with old-time families who told stories of going fishing near Green and Rattlesnake Islands. They told us, "If we made noises on the rocky shores, we could hear the rattle of the rattlesnakes."

The Lake Erie water snakes continue to be very numerous on the islands. They are found everywhere, but mainly closer to the water and among the rocks of the shoreline. They are often seen swimming or sunning on rocks and on boat swim platforms. They feed on small fish, small birds, frogs, and salamanders, and they give birth to an average of twenty-five young snakes that are born alive at seven to nine inches long. The young are not cared for, and upon birth, must find their own way in the world.

This non-poisonous snake is very aggressive and will continue to strike until totally exhausted. I met one coiled on the driveway,

*More than sixty archeological sites have been discovered on Kelleys Island, some with inscriptions 12,000 years old.*

# "We found our extensive experience with small boats on Sage Lake helped make the transition to the Great Lakes waters less stressful than we expected."

and as I slowly drove by, it continued to strike the front and rear car tires. Our neighbor kept a jet ski on the rear swim platform of his boat, and once when removing the jet ski's canvas cover, he was bitten three times by a large Lake Erie water snake. He rushed to the hospital to receive aid to avoid an infection.

Lake Erie is renowned for its great commercial and sport fishing industries. Its freshwater lake perch, walleye (Canadian pickerel), bass, sturgeon, and numerous other freshwater fish are served on menus world-wide. Anglers come to Lake Erie, trailering their own boat or paying to go on a "head boat," a large boat carrying a group of fishermen and fisherwomen. At the so-called "magic spot," the captain lowers an anchor, and everyone drops their fishing lines (normally baited with minnows) to the bottom of the lake. Elaine had a magic touch and usually caught more fish than yours truly. In the 1990s, each person could legally keep ninety perch per day. Today the limit in most areas is reduced to thirty per day.

Cleaning fish can be effortless if you take them to a fish-cleaning company with a descaling machine and talented human cutters, who are extremely proficient and quick at slicing off beautiful fillets. Of course, I had the chore of cleaning the boat and gear. However, after a lot of practice, I found the reward for doing all this hard work.

It came about as soon as I sat down and began eating those Lake Erie mouth-watering deep-fried perch or pan-fried walleye, so carefully prepared by Elaine.

## OUR FIRST GREAT LAKES VESSEL

We began our acquaintance with Lake Erie when we bought our first 290 Sea Ray Sundancer in April 1992. It was thirty-two feet in length, with an eight-foot beam. We intended the boat to be our weekend home, whether we were cruising to distant locations or relaxing quietly at our dock in the marina.

Propulsion was provided by a single big-block V-8 in the bilge that was connected through the transom to an out-drive. The outdrive pivoted to steer the boat and the drive shaft to rotate the propeller, moving the boat forward or in reverse.

The first thing we had to learn was a new vocabulary for the boat. The bedroom was a stateroom, the toilet a head, the kitchen a galley, but a shower was a shower.

The Sea Ray was equipped with a forward stateroom with a double bed, storage under the bed, and a closet. A head with a sink and toilet stool were located in the shower. A bunk with a sliding curtain was at the rear of the galley for additional seating and sleeping for visitors.

The galley was fitted with an under-the-counter refrigerator powered by a twelve-volt battery, or 120 volts when connected to shore power. Only 120-volt shore power heated the double burner stove top and microwave. A movable dining table sat in front of a fixed bench seat accommodating up to four people.

We made a decision not to fry any food in the galley. Most marinas have cooking grills for such special meal preparation.

The boat had a 120-volt shore-powered hot water heater. The hot water was also heated by the engine when the boat was underway, so when we returned to port, we had hot water. We filled our fifty-gallon freshwater tank whenever fresh water was available at marinas.

All the shower and galley sink water went directly into the lake, so we were very careful about how much soap or dirty water we deposited into the lake.

The toilet used a vacuum system for moving the toilet water into a forty-gallon wastewater tank. The sewage had to be pumped out at the dock where gas was purchased or at a special sewage disposal station.

The lower engine compartment, rearward from the aft bunk area, included the V-8 engine attached to the outdrive through the transom, freshwater tank, hot water heater, sewage-holding tank, power-steering pump, two twelve-volt batteries, electrical 120-volt supply from shore power, double bilge pumps, and hydraulic-operated trim tabs.

Our favorite location on the boat was the open topside area. A retractable canvas cover was attached to the windshield and stretched the entire length of the upper area, with eisenglass side and aft curtains. The helm area encompassed the steering wheel, single lever throttle and shift control, trim tab switches, light switches, VHF radio and external antenna, compass, RPM indicator, gauges, Raynav 580 Loran C readout display and antenna, and light controls for day and night use. The captain and first mate had a single bench seat, and an aft bench seat was reserved for guests or naps.

The Treasure Cove sales and service team made certain we became familiar with all the features of the vessel and gave us on-the-water training to acquaint us with the Sea Ray's features, capabilities, and limitations.

We found our extensive experience with small boats on Sage Lake helped make the transition to the Great Lakes waters less stressful than we expected. However, the wide open waters created higher winds and waves, and the frequent boat traffic required more attention.

I wanted to be able to experience, overcome, and anticipate every possible situation before being faced with an actual catastrophe, so I embarked on each new challenge as a learning opportunity. This is the way I had lived my early life, and I was determined Elaine and I were going to be mentally and physically ready for this new life on the water. Our process of learning and familiarizing ourselves with the first Great Lake was, as I tell friends, "awe-inspiring and yet a real challenge."

Elaine quickly demonstrated skills in detecting debris in the water as we cruised at higher speeds. She could easily identify floating trees, docks, and trash, but her sharp eyes also found fish nets and markers—and, I would guess, anything else that could possibly float.

Commercial fishermen place their gill nets vertical to the nearest shore; this practice is true in American and Canadian waters. The outer end is marked with two flags on a vertical pole, and the inner end (shore end) is marked with a shorter pole with one flag. The nets may be staggered at various distances from shore, requiring boaters to change directions to find the end of the net. Passing over a net is extremely risky, since the top line holding the net in the vertical position is usually near the surface. If a boat becomes entangled and damages the net, you will have to pay big bucks to the net owner and possibly damage your drive system. You may even require a tow.

When northeasterly winds accompany storms, the water from the eastern part of Lake Erie is blown into the western basin, causing what is called the Erie Tide. Depending on wind speed and duration, water levels will increase several feet, creating huge waves and flooding. It took us some time to learn how to tie off the boat so sudden water level changes wouldn't damage the boat.

Over our twenty-five years on Lake Erie, I heard stories about western basin waves becoming so high that the lake bottom sand was

# "When piloting a boat on the Great Lakes, the rules of the road are specifically defined for areas where no markers are available to provide a set path."

glimpsed between the waves. Thank goodness we were never caught in this situation, but we always carefully monitored the weather forecast.

Likewise with strong westerly winds, the western basin lake levels drop as water is blown out. Catawba Island is now a peninsula located in the western basin, surrounded by Lake Erie on its east, north, and west sides. In our years on Lake Erie, we only experienced a couple feet of lower water in the western basin, although we had to be alert if we were cruising over shoals and normal low-water areas.

We very quickly learned that the waves on Lake Erie differ from those on other Great Lakes. If you've seen one wave, you haven't seen them all. So true! During my years of experience, I became convinced that the most difficult waves "to make way on" are the Lake Erie waves. They form quickly due to the lake's east-west orientation and shallow depths. Erie's waves are closer together and are shaped with a sharper entrance into a wave, while the backside drop-off is steeper. Thus, the ride is much rougher, and travel times are significantly extended.

When a wave is moving toward a boat, the basic maneuver is to enter the wave at about a forty-five-degree angle and attempt to turn back when on the back side of the wave. On Lake Erie, this is often impossible, as the boat is already entering into the next wave before you are able to turn back.

In our later years of boating, when we were moving yachts for boat-building companies, we often encountered eight-foot Lake Erie waves that made it nearly impossible to keep the boat propellers in the water. Entering the wave had to be attempted at a much smaller angle, and there was little opportunity to turn back to quarter the next wave at the same angle.

On a trip to Erie, Pennsylvania, our forty-mile voyage along the south shore of Lake Erie took us four hours. Under more reasonable seas, it would have been one-and-one-half hours. The nor'easter winds created the typical close sequence of Lake Erie waves, but we were facing waves as high as eight feet at forty-five degrees to our desired direction. That day, we had to enter the waves at even a smaller angle than normal, and half the time we were heading toward the southern shore rather than eastward. In order to make headway eastward, we had to turn north toward the center of the lake, then return to quartering the waves as we again moved toward shore. This maneuvering made little forward progress toward Erie. A long and tiring day.

### OVERCOMING THE FEAR OF LOSING SIGHT OF LAND

In the early 1990s, the technology supporting navigation was in the process of monumental changes. We ordered our first Sea Ray with the latest Raymarine Loran C technology, which was developed prior to World War II, and used to provide an approximate location for vessels on the water. X and Y directionally separate hyperbola short-wave radio waves are sent out from land and are collected by the Loran C antenna on the boat. The boat's position is identified as an X and Y display on the Loran C monitor. Finding the intersection of the X and Y lines on the paper chart identifies the boat's approximate

*The Blue Water Bridge stretches between Port Huron and Sarnia, the entrance into Lake Huron. In July 1992, two months after purchasing our first Great Lakes boat, we set off to explore Lake Huron.*

position. If the boat is moving, it identifies where the boat was located when the data was received.

In July of 1992, only two months after receiving our first Great Lakes boat, we accumulated the charts for Lake Erie, Lake St. Clair, Detroit River, St. Clair River, and Lake Huron for planning our first adventure on Lake Huron. Our purpose was to cruise far from land and then find our way to a specific place. Boating on Lake Erie didn't provide an opportunity to get out of sight of land long enough to really test if we knew what we were doing, right or wrong.

We also wanted to practice and properly communicate using the VHF (very high frequency) radio with call letters, boat name, and correct rules of communication. We understood the rules of the road, but we had to experience the many actual signs, colors, and visual markers required to maneuver on open water with many boats traveling in different directions.

We had already experienced the absolute necessity of being highly diligent on watch as we cruised Lake Erie. Logs and other debris are most prevalent there, since the lake is the collection point of everything floating from Lake Superior, Lake Huron, Lake Michigan, St. Clair River, Lake St. Clair, and the Detroit River. Added to these impediments are the vast number of fish nets in both the American and Canadian waters of Lake Erie. Elaine became particularly adept at spotting debris and fish nets, so in all our years on the water, we never became entangled in a fish net.

Since I was always asking questions—one of my original characteristics—I set up a meeting with John, the manager/owner of Treasure Cove Marina, to review our intended cruise onto Lake Huron. He studied the entire path we would take up the Detroit River, Lake St Clair, and the St. Clair River, while pointing out areas where we needed to watch carefully for markers and shallow areas.

He also warned us about the danger of meeting and passing a lake freighter. "Avoid getting too close to a moving freighter," he emphasized. "Its wake could suck your boat into the steel side of the freighter, possibly sinking your boat. This is a very dangerous situation."

We took his words to heart.

Now ready and prepared, we motored across Lake Erie and entered the Livingston Shipping Channel at the Detroit River Lighthouse. Immediately, we met a lake freighter in the channel. Thanks to the critically important advice from John, we kept our distance and safely passed by our first lake freighter.

Breathing somewhat easier, we continued, watching for debris in the water, keeping the green markers on the port (left) side, and red markers on the starboard (right) side. That is the international standard for vessels returning from the sea, or in this case, going upstream from the Atlantic Ocean.

The vessel traffic was continuous, and in some areas even congested. We began to appreciate the importance of this waterway from Lake Erie to Lake Huron in supporting commerce. The traffic ranged from freighters to private power boats, sailboats, fishing boats, and even ferries crossing between U.S.A. and Canada. Ferries have special privileges, such as no-wake areas (meaning your vessel shouldn't produce a wave as you pass by). They also have complete right-of-way.

When piloting a boat on the Great Lakes, the rules of the road are specifically defined for areas where no markers are available to provide a set path. All boaters should know and practice these rules when on open water, but not all do. We received this training when we were certified in the sailing class we took in Bay City. Specific rules apply for meeting, passing, or crossing another boat's apparent path.

Growing up in the forests of the Upper Peninsula of Michigan, I learned to use a compass as a basic skill. On the water, wind, currents, and waves cause constant changes to a boat's location, so corrections are always required. However, if a captain has the ability to receive position data and can identify it on the chart, he or she can make adjustments to bring the boat back onto the desired path.

Safely arriving at the entrance to Lake Huron, we followed the marked shipping channel out into the lake. Losing sight of land, we continued in a northerly direction, since our goal was to cruise at least fifty miles north of Port Huron and travel somewhere in the center of the lake. Our final destination was Port Sanilac, on the western shore of Lake Huron.

Fortunately, we chose a perfect day, as the lake only had a light chop and the marine forecast was for waves of one to two feet. Checking the Loran data for a readout, we identified our location on our chart. From that approximate point, we defined a compass heading to Port Sanilac harbor and set the boat on that course. I will admit I had some apprehension, but always knew that if we headed in a westerly direction, we would eventually reach the shore of Michigan, even if we didn't know where exactly.

When we saw the Michigan shoreline and simultaneously the Port Sanilac entrance marker to the harbor, we celebrated with high fives and hugs, as we were right on target. We had achieved our first major step in our career of cruising on the Great Lakes.

We then used our VHF radio to call the Port Sanilac harbormaster to obtain a dock for the night. With all these accomplishments, we celebrated by indulging in an outstanding dinner at the Port Sanilac Sailing Club.

The next morning, we followed the shoreline south to Lexington Harbor, obtained a temporary dock, and walked into town to enjoy a hamburger at Wimpy's Diner with Popeye the Sailor Man. This was a new way for us to enjoy traveling: finding new and interesting towns, historical spots, parks, marinas, and restaurants. "This is going to be a fun—and challenging—way to live." Elaine exclaimed. I agreed.

> "The flashing lightning enveloped the boat like a giant fire ball, while extremely sharp claps of thunder rang rapidly in our ears. A sudden thought hit me: could we be hit by lightning?"

Of course, we still had a lot to learn. We hadn't experienced stormy weather and rough seas in order to truly develop the skills necessary to navigate on the Great Lakes—but we didn't have to wait very long. In fact, it was the same day.

Returning to Lake Erie after our first northern cruise to Lake Huron, we stopped to peer out into the lake from the protected waters of the Detroit River. We were stunned to see a huge thunderstorm directly south of us. Holding our position in the river current, we discussed the options of returning up river and finding dockage for the night or taking on the storm.

The storm appeared to be moving quite rapidly east along the south shore of the lake, then at least twenty miles away. Looking to the west, we could see the clear skies at the western end of the storm. The clouds were very high, and occasional lightning flashed across the sky. As we waited and contemplated the overnight option, I observed the storm moving very fast.

In my very limited wisdom, I told Elaine, 'That's a fast-moving storm. It will most likely move beyond Catawba Island by the time we arrive home. Look, we can even see the the clear weather at the back end of the storm."

"Let's hope and pray you know what you're doing!" was her reply.

So we began our journey into Lake Erie. The storm was creating increased winds and we were beginning to experience some larger waves as we continued our southeasterly course to Catawba Island.

All of a sudden, I realized the storm had turned north, and we were heading straight into it. I will admit I felt my first real panic on the Great Lakes with a thunderstorm engulfing our very tiny boat.

As I turned the bow into the waves, Elaine retreated into a fetal position on the forward bench seat next to me. The thunderstorm swallowed and surrounded us with lighting, wind, and rain. As our bow disappeared into the Lake Erie thunderstorm, the high wind carried a wall of water and seemed to stop the boat's forward movement. Next, the downpour struck. I wasn't able to see beyond a minimal distance in front of us. Oh, if only we had radar to see what is actually in front of us, I told myself.

The flashing lightning enveloped the boat like a giant fire ball, while extremely sharp claps of thunder rang rapidly in our ears. A sudden thought hit me: could we be hit by lightning? Sea Ray's documentation stated the boat was properly grounded, but what about the five-foot VHF antenna sticking straight up above us? Without hesitation, I opened the canvas, went out into the downpour of what felt like buckets of water being thrown at me, and lowered the antenna.

I had determined our location on the charts before we entered the storm, so I didn't worry about running into land. I kept the boat headed directly into the wind, and three or four more periods of blinding lightning enveloped us, followed by those deafening claps of thunder. The downpour of heavy rain and wind followed the

*Boat traffic was brisk on a perfect day like this.*

thunder and lightning, causing the rain to pour through any and all minute openings in the canvas covering. During a pause in the storm, I changed the compass heading to bring us back on our planned path. We had been blown to the east of our desired path, and a lull in the wind and rain allowed us to relax for a moment.

The cloud cover made it difficult to know more about the storm, but seeing an approaching wall of rain, I yelled, "Here it comes again!" We were engulfed by the full fierceness of the rain, lightning, and thunder.

Elaine went into another fetal position, while I tried to keep the bow into the waves. But lightning surrounded the boat, and sharp thunder clapped over and over. It seemed to continue forever, until the clouds finally broke and we glimpsed the sun. What a relief! We were alive! Surprised, we could see our distant marina entrance and HOME.

As I prepared to dock our boat, the elderly gentleman everyone called The Mayor walked toward us on the dock.

"You must have come through the thunderstorms," he commented in a John Wayne voice.

Elaine appeared relieved and was back to her normal exuberant self as she stood on the dock, water streaming from her wet hair. "We just came through two thunderstorms! It was a horrible experience!" Elaine exclaimed. "The lighting and thunder enveloped the boat and us. It rained so hard that our canvas top leaked. I'm soaking wet." She waved her arms to shake off the water.

The Mayor grinned, "It seems that you have. Based on what I see looking at you, I think we need to organize a wet T-shirt contest in the near future."

## NIGHT CRUISING

Operating a boat at night isn't for the faint-hearted. In a normal situation, eyes will automatically adapt to darkness in a relatively short time. But after your eyes have adapted to night vision and are suddenly struck with a bright light, you will require at least forty-five minutes before night vision returns. Therefore, all experienced captains know to avoid bright lights in the dark. Otherwise, the result can be catastrophic.

I know a captain who regularly used a spotlight to search for his dock until one night when a U.S. Coast Guard boat was docked nearby and he flashed the beam at their boat. The entire Coast Guard crew was out of commission for forty-five minutes, due to their loss of night vision. Thank goodness they weren't needed for a rescue in that time period, as that captain would have suffered much stiffer penalties. The Coast Guard crew, however, used the forty-five minutes to prepare a huge ticket for the delinquent captain. (By the way, a boat helm light is usually red, to reduce this from happening.)

## THE FORCED FIRST NIGHT CRUISE

In 1994, we upgraded ELEANA and purchased a used 370 Sea Ray Express Cruiser, which had twin big-block V-8's, one stateroom, radar, Global Positioning System (GPS) Chart Plotter, and VHF radio.

*Owning a Sea Ray was just a dream during our early married years—but, in time, the dream became a reality.*

> "Exiting the channel, I made the turn to head toward home. We were now in complete blackness. The women began to panic, but Elaine tried to console them—to no avail."

GPS uses a satellite or satellites to accurately locate the boat's position on the surface of the lake and mark the boat's location on the navigation chart that is displayed on the computer screen—a very simple system in today's world. GPS was new at the time, however, and replaced the Loran C for navigation. We spent many hours to become comfortable with GPS and, more importantly, to rely on it. Many mariners remained skeptical of the new technology and kept their Loran C's for a while.

One afternoon, we asked two other couples if they wanted to join us for a one-and-one-half hour, thirty-mile cruise to a new restaurant on the Maumee River in downtown Toledo. The day was gorgeous, perfect for cruising, and the weather forecast called for clear skies and no wind. The plan was to depart at 4:30, with a dinner reservation for six o'clock, allowing us plenty of time to return before dark.

We departed as planned, but very soon we began to encounter numerous fish nets, all placed vertically to the shore line. As soon as we followed a net away from the shore and turned around the outer flag pole toward Toledo, we immediately faced another net. They were staggered closer together and farther from shore. One net, broken or cut in half, had drifted in many different directions. We managed to avoid entangling the boat propellers in the net, but we were now way behind our intended plan.

Another delay occurred as we entered Toledo's dredged shipping lane between Lake Erie and the Maumee River entrance. Because of the shallow water adjacent to the shipping lane, we had to stay in the shipping lane and wait for outbound and inbound freighters to meet and clear each other.

We finally arrived at the restaurant at seven o'clock, and fortunately found an open dock directly in front of the restaurant.

A waitress arrived and informed us we wouldn't be seated until eight o'clock. However, she took our drink and appetizer orders, and we remained onboard. All of us relaxed, sitting on ELEANA and enjoying the chance to watch the river's boat traffic and the sun sinking beyond the city buildings.

Even though we hadn't ordered dinner, I asked everyone if they wanted to return home, but the consensus was to stay and enjoy the evening. I think a few were having a great time and didn't realize that we would be returning in the dark. I actually was ecstatic to be able to travel on the water in darkness, relying on the onboard radar technology. One of the friends told me, "We all have confidence in your skills. And besides, the boat has radar on board."

We were finally underway after nine o'clock, following a delicious meal. I was excited to turn on the radar for my first night run on Lake Erie. Plus, I had two experienced boaters for assistance, even if they had never used radar. The support was comforting, to have additional eyes on the radar while others watched for ships' lights to verify if the blip on the radar really was a ship. My initial apprehension was considerably reduced.

My plan was to take the shipping channel out to the end, which would put us farther from home and at the mid-lake position in the western basin. We most likely would be the only boat at the center of the lake.

I asked the guys to call out the channel can numbers as we passed by, so I could verify where we were in the channel on the chart plotter. The women wanted to use flashlights to light the cans, but I explained night vision issues.

Exiting the channel, I made the turn to head toward home. We were now in complete blackness. The women began to panic, but Elaine tried to console them—to no avail. They wanted lights, and they were concerned about other boats.

All vessels are required to have a red light on the port side (left), a green light on the starboard side (right), and a small white light on top of the mast, located at the center of the boat's highest roof. I asked everyone to be on the lookout for red, green, and/or small white masthead lights.

"What if we run into land?" one of the women asked.

I suggested everyone view the radar screen, which was showing the distant outlines of land and not showing any blips indicating other boats on the lake. This seemed to calm everyone, and we returned without incident.

I was now confident of my ability to handle night travel on the water if I were suddenly required to do so. I felt so good when Elaine praised me for my performance and assured me that she was confident we could handle night cruising, if necessary. Another check mark on my list of things to experience and be prepared for.

However, as we exited the boat, I heard the wives tell their husbands, as they walked into the night, "NEVER AGAIN!"

## NAVIGATION ON WATER

In order to navigate on the Great Lakes, I had to perfect my compass knowledge. I grew up using a compass to hunt and navigate through a deer yard study in the Porcupine Mountains. In the study, we had to track all our movements and return to our starting point using the compass and measuring the distances we walked in each direction.

Using a compass on the land is easy, but a knowledgeable boater relying on paper charts and compass must, in my opinion, know more of what is being used and what is printed on paper.

All National Oceanic and Atmospheric Administration Great Lakes charts (NOAA) indicate a "true" heading to a specific location on the paper chart. True is established from the northern tip of the rotating axis of the earth on the northern hemisphere. It is a fixed and specific point on a chart.

All compasses point to the North Pole, the magnetic position of the North Pole. But the North Pole is not on the axis point of the earth's rotation. Rather, it is a significant distance from the axis point, a fact that all boaters should be aware of.

If you're reading a compass on the east end of Lake Erie, the compass reading is 10.5 degrees less than True North, and if you are at the west end of the lake it is only 6.5 degrees from True North. This difference could affect the boat's real path in relation to the chart's True position direction.

When using a chart with a True degree direction definition, the boater must also know the compass correction factor at that point where the boat is located, to avoid grounding or hitting underwater obstacles. A lesson I learned well. ∎

LAKE HURON
GEORGIAN BAY
NORTH CHANNEL
MANITOULIN ISLAND
BRUCE PENINSULA
SAGINAW BAY
NOTTAWASAGA BAY
MICHIGAN
ONTARIO
Manitoulin Basin
Six Fathom Scarp
Ipperwash Scarp
Six Fathom Bank
Deepest Sounding
CANADA
UNITED STATES
LAKE NIPISSING
STRAITS OF MACKINAC
Mackinac I
Bois Blanc I
Cheboygan
Petoskey
Hammond Bay Harbor
Forty Mile Pt
Rogers City
Calcite Harbor
Presque Isle
Stoneport
Grand Lake
Middle I
Rockport
Thunder Bay
Thunder Bay I
North Point
Alpena
Ossineke
South Pt
Hubbard Lake
Sturgeon Pt
Harrisville
Au Sable River
Oscoda
Au Sable Pt
Tawas City
Tawas Pt
Alabaster
Port Austin Reef
Pte aux Barques
Port Austin
Charity I
Pt au Gres
Port Crescent
Caseville
Sand Pt
Port Hope
Harbor Beach
Bay Port
Sebewaing
Fish Pt
BAY CITY
SAGINAW
Port Sanilac
Lexington
Lakeport
PORT HURON
Marysville
St Clair
SARNIA
Point Edward
Corunna
Courtright
Kettle Pt
Cape Ipperwash
Port Franks
Grand Bend
Bayfield
Goderich
Port Albert
Point Clark
Kincardine
Macpherson Pt
Port Elgin
Southampton
Owen Sound
Wiarton
Meaford
Collingwood
Thornbury
Barrie
Midland
Christian I
Parry Sound
Depot Harbour
Byng Inlet
Pte au Baril
Key Harbour
Killarney
Little Current
Gore Bay
Cockburn Island
Drummond Island
De Tour Village
St Joseph Island
Bruce Mines
Thessalon
Blind River
Serpent River
Spanish River
French River
Cabot Head
Cape Hurd
Tobermory
Fishing Islands
Fitzwilliam I
Main Channel
Halfmoon I
Lonely I
Western Is
Sandy I
HAMILTON
Burlington
Port Credit
Oakville
Bronte
Clarkson
Nanticoke
Port Dover
Port Maitland
BUFFALO
DETROIT
LAKE ST CLAIR
GRAND RAPIDS
Navigation and power diversion
Power diversion

## CHAPTER 5
# Lake Huron: "The Fresh-water Sea"

IN 1961, on one of our three honeymoon days on Mackinac Island, we sat on a marble bench on the hillside below Fort Mackinac, looking down onto the marina filled with gleaming pleasure craft. I promised Elaine, "One day we're going to have our boat in this marina." I recall how she smiled, looked into my eyes, and nodded.

When Elaine and I married in June of that year, Elaine's uncle and aunt gave us a week's use of a cottage on Ocqueoc Lake, just west and north of Rogers City, which is located near the shore of Lake Huron. On three separate days, we drove to Mackinaw City and boarded a ferry to spend the day and early evening on Mackinac Island. Over our sixty-two years of marriage, we stretched the truth by saying that we honeymooned on Mackinac Island—without adding that we were there on three separate days.

Before the arrival of Europeans, as many as 25,000 indigenous Huron people lived and fished along the shores of the second-largest of the Great Lakes (according to NOAA Great Lakes Chart-14500). Huron is the world's fourth-largest body of fresh water. In 1615, French explorer Samuel de Champlain became the first European to explore the lake, which the French initially called La Mer Douce, "The Freshwater Sea," and later, Lac Huron.

Throughout its history, the lake has presented challenges—some of them deadly—to boats and sailors. On November 9, 1913 alone, a severe storm raged across the lake, claiming the lives of 235 sailors and sinking ten ships. Historians estimate that more than one thousand ships lie buried in its lake bed.

Lake Huron and Lake Michigan have the same level of water and are only connected by the five-mile-wide Straits of Mackinac. The combined surface area of Lake Huron and Lake Michigan creates the largest freshwater lake in the world. Lake Huron covers 51,700 square miles, with a maximum depth of 752 feet, shallower than Lake Michigan's 925 feet.

Other than watershed rivers and streams, the incoming water entering Lake Huron is the excess water from Lake Michigan passing through the Straits of Mackinac and St. Marys River, the only outlet from Lake Superior. Environmentalists suggest that the total water capacity of Lake Huron is replaced in twenty-two years. My experienced opinion is that it is primarily due to two factors: Lake Huron is shallower than Lake Michigan, and the St. Clair River is five feet lower than the lake. In my personal experience, exiting Lake Huron into the St. Clair River in a boat requires special care, since a tremendous amount of water passes through the narrow opening into the river.

Canada and Michigan share Lake Huron, with the border dividing St. Marys River and continuing into and down the St. Clair River to Lake St. Clair, which is also shared between the two nations. In my terms, Lake St. Clair is very shallow, "a wide place in

# "The waters of Lake Huron north of Thunder Bay are regarded as the most treacherous stretch of water within the Great Lakes."

the St. Clair River." The border then continues to divide the Detroit River as it flows into Lake Erie.

To me, Lake Huron consists of three different seas: Canada's Georgian Bay, Canada's North Channel, and Michigan's Saginaw Bay. Each of these seas has characteristics that set them apart and present different challenges.

As I studied historical information about October and November storms and their waves on the Great Lakes, I read about thirty-five-foot waves joining into one wave twice as high. In this book, I only describe our encounters with summer storms and times when we were stranded in port to avoid serious storms.

## LAKE HURON ADVENTURE

In July of 1994, I convinced Elaine we should go to Mackinac Island on our ELEANA and spend time in the Mackinac Island Marina to fulfill the commitment I made to her thirty-three years earlier.

We departed from our dock at Treasure Cove Marina on Lake Erie for our three-hundred-mile cruise across Lake Erie, up the Detroit River, through Lake St. Clair, and up St. Clair River. We entered Lake Huron after passing under the Blue Water Bridge connecting the U.S.A. and Canada.

We took a few minutes before entering Lake Huron to stop and view the docked Light Ship No. 3, the HURON, one of only a few remaining original U.S. light ships from the 1820s. In this time period, light ships were used to mark dangerous areas where lighthouses were impossible to construct. The HURON served as the light ship marking the entrance into the six-mile, twenty-four-foot-deep channel from Lake Huron into the St. Clair River.

Can you imagine the character of the individuals who maintained this floating lighthouse, enduring storms with huge twelve-foot waves?

Our first cruise to Mackinac Island was uneventful. The weather was beautiful, and we enjoyed only one- or two-foot waves throughout the entire two weeks. Our first stop was Port Sanilac, where we had previously stayed. Our second stop was Harrisville, which, in the future, became a regular stop because of its scenic harbor, facilities, and outstanding local restaurant that provided transportation from and to the marina.

Approaching Presque Isle Marina, we encountered a new challenge. We had to use land-based range markers to locate the final entrance into the marina. The first vertical marker was thirty-five feet high. The second, located farther on the land, was fifty feet high. Lining up these makers provided a safe route for us to follow into the bay. Once farther into the bay, we found the normal red and green cans marking the channel into the large Presque Isle Marina, which is considered the best Lake Huron "harbor of refuge" for pleasure craft.

Once we secured our boat, we visited the Old Presque Isle Lighthouse, which locals claim to be haunted. One of the oldest surviving lighthouses on the Great Lakes, it was built in 1840 to a height of thirty feet, with a diameter of eighteen feet at the base. The bottom two-thirds of the lighthouse was constructed of stone, with a round brick section above. In 1870, after building the new 113-foot Presque Isle Lighthouse, the old was abandoned.

As we climbed up the original lighthouse, we found the ancient Fresnel lens still in place. The base was said to rotate at certain times and conditions. But did that occur only when ghostly hands were at work?

From inside the lighthouse, I specifically looked at the direction the light was pointed. Later, as I stood outside on the circular walkway, I looked back to discover that the whole light had moved from my inside view and was now pointing directly at me. I won't say whether or not I believe in ghosts, but I will admit we couldn't get back to the ground fast enough.

Departing Presque Isle Harbor, our next challenge was to cruise around the Thunder Bay National Marine Sanctuary and Shipwreck Alley, immediately north of the Thunder Bay entrance. The sanctuary protects nearly one hundred shipwrecks representing two centuries of Great Lakes shipping, as well as the stories of the sailors and merchants who went down with the ships.

The Michigan shoreline turns northwest here. All vessels, whether north or southbound, must make a turn around this area.

Thunder Bay's opening from Lake Huron is approximately twelve miles wide, and the village of Thunder Bay is located at the northwestern tip of the bay, approximately nine miles from the lake.

The waters of Lake Huron north of Thunder Bay are regarded as the most treacherous stretch of water within the Great Lakes. Three islands, huge rocks, and shoals extend into the lake at least seven miles from the curving shoreline.

Maritime historians suggest that winds and currents have been responsible for two hundred shipwrecks in this area, most of them occurring in November, when unpredictable weather, murky fog banks, sudden gales, and rocky shoals threaten ships.

I have read about the era when sailing ships were gradually replaced by steam-powered ships. In order to carry additional ore or grain from the west end of Lake Superior, the northbound steam-powered ships would tow an empty sailing ship without sails (called a consort), and thereby move more tonnage to market upon their return.

When a northbound steam-powered ship towing an empty consort reached this area, a turn to port is required to go around the land. When strong winds blew from the south, they could push the empty sailing consort directly north, ahead of the slow steamer, thus causing collisions and even the sinking of vessels.

We were warned to stay well outside the Sanctuary area, as boulders the size of a house lurk just under the surface of the water. They can become a greater hazard if larger waves are present. Also beneath the surface are shipwrecks ranging from nineteenth-century wooden side-wheeler paddle steamers to twentieth-century steel-hulled steamers. We definitely didn't want to add ELEANA or some of our outdrive parts to the pile.

As we cruised on the eastern side of the Sanctuary, we passed by a huge steel side of a shipwreck on the outer boundary of the Sanctuary. The wreck projected about twenty to thirty feet out of the water and had a beacon maker on top. Researching for information, we found that it was the NORDMEER, a foreign 471-foot steel ocean cargo freighter that was wrecked in 1966. We found it sitting on a boulder in forty feet of water. During our travels past the NORDMEER over the following seventeen years, we observed less and less of the vessel, as it slowly decomposed in the open air.

Our next stop was Mackinaw City on the Straits of Mackinac, the last stop on Michigan's Lower Peninsula before crossing over into the rugged and beautiful Upper Peninsula.

A native of Michigan, and in particular the Upper Peninsula, I was well aware of the difference in the spelling of Mackinac and Mackinaw even though both names are pronounced with "aw" at the end.

The Ojibwa called the area "Mitchimakinak," which translates to "big turtle," referring to the distant shape of Mackinac Island. The French spelling called for a "c" at the end. The British not only shortened the Ojibwa name, but spelled the city's name with an "aw," although all other sites—the island, bridge, and straits—retain the French "c." Mackinac Island, Mackinac Bridge, and Straits of Mackinac.

To arrive at the Mackinaw City Marina, we passed between Bois Blanc Island and Cheboygan, where we first became acquainted with Lake Huron fog. As we approached the location where we had crossed between Bois Blanc and Cheboygan twenty-five years earlier through a solid fog bank in a much smaller boat, we relived that harrowing six-mile fog-bound crossing.

*Elaine sits on a very special Mackinac Island bench. Thirty-three years earlier, while sitting together there, I promised her that one day we would return with our own boat and dock it in the island's marina.*

In Mackinaw City, the harbormaster explained the procedures for obtaining a dock on Mackinac Island. We had to be in the Mackinac Island Harbor ready to call the harbormaster at seven o'clock in the morning in order to register for a dock. We followed these instructions, and the island harbormaster informed us to stay in the harbor and wait for a VHF call to direct us to our assigned dock.

In the normal turnover of dockage, boaters can only stay at Mackinac Island's marina a maximum of four nights and must leave before eleven o'clock in the morning. Fortunately, our notification came early, and we were placed on a shore dock right in front of Fort Mackinac and the white marble bench. After docking, tying off, and connecting shore power, we quickly walked up the hill to sit on what we believed to be the same well-worn white marble bench. As we sat there, we relived our honeymoon memories and my commitment to have our own boat right here where the ELEANA was docked, a promise I made thirty-three years earlier.

Our honeymoon experiences on Mackinac Island made it easy to explore the old haunts we had enjoyed before. We found many more intriguing stores and restaurants—and this time we were able to afford them. Upon our departure from Mackinac Island, we thanked the Lord for this wonderful adventure and unique experience.

With the weather continuing to be sunny and warm and the seas calm, we decided to further extend our exploration of Lake Huron by going to Hessel on Michigan's Upper Peninsula. It was a gorgeous morning as we departed from Mackinac Island on the ten-mile ride to Hessel. Since we arrived so early in the day, the harbormaster quickly said, "Just pick a dock you like."

It so happened that Hessel has a wonderful bakery with outstanding donuts, which we certainly enjoyed that morning with coffee. Today Hessel is home to the Les Cheneaux Culinary School, which I believe is the extension of the old excellent bakery.

That morning the harbor became busy as Hessel's local people were preparing for the yearly World's Largest Antique Wooden Boat Show. Some beautiful old woodies were being launched, and we had an opportunity to admire their craftsmanship and beauty as we talked to the owners.

Hessel is located on the western edge of the Les Cheneaux Islands, an archipelago of thirty-six islands located along twelve miles of Lake Huron's north shore, east of the Straits of Mackinac. Only one island is open to the public, Government Island, which is only accessible by boat. All the other islands are inhabited. The waterways are properly marked and maintained, so boaters must be aware of depth, as the narrows between the islands can be hazardous.

Our next destination was Detour, Michigan, located on the St. Marys River, which is the outlet of Lake Superior, and ends in Lake Huron. Detour's history dates back to an ancient Ojibwa settlement that later became a center for the natives' fur trade with France.

Upon awakening the next morning on ELEANA, we found the fog was so thick that we were unable to see across the small marina. I talked to the harbormaster, who informed us that it was projected to continue and possibly lift later in the day.

Wow, an opportunity to experience fog, and on our planned course! Another condition to overcome fear and improve our boating capability while continuing our cruise.

Elaine suggested we should wait for it to lift. "I remember the last time we entered fog on Lake Huron, and I don't need another repeat performance!"

I listened, but I explained my logic: "We need to experience fog in an area where we will very likely be the only boat, because no marinas exist between Hessel and our destination. Also, there won't be any lake freighters because we won't be near their shipping lanes." I even showed her on the chart where the shipping lanes exist and where we would be going.

Elaine finally agreed to go. So I prepared the ELEANA to depart and reviewed what Elaine needed to do as a lookout. She was also in charge of handling the paper chart for me and operating the fog warning sound with our boat horn.

I plotted our course to Detour, about forty miles east of our location. We were underway by nine o'clock in the morning, and I was convinced we would have a late lunch in Detour.

Our 290 Sea Ray Sundancer didn't have radar or a chart plotter, so we had to use the data from the Raynav 580 Loran C device and make certain we were near or on the course I had designed. Everything was going according to plan as we slowly traveled at approximately eight miles per hour through the fog.

In order to avoid a number of shoals, I had planned to head on a more southerly course before turning to the northeast, thereby staying south of Martin Reef Light. As we made our way through the thick fog, Elaine was sounding our fog horn on the prescribed timing: a prolonged blast about five seconds long every two minutes. Our visibility improved a little, and we could see about twenty yards ahead.

*A goal fulfilled: docking my own boat at the Mackinac Island Marina.*

I was particularly worried about staying south of the Martin Reef, which is located four miles south of the Upper Peninsula shoreline. Constructed right on the shoal it marks, Martin Reef Lighthouse is a beautiful square white limestone structure that has recently been purchased by a private party.

Using the chart and Loran C, I had confirmed we had passed south of Martin Reef and were on our way to Detour when I noticed the depth sounder reading sixty to seventy feet. We had just been running in depths of three hundred to four hundred feet. With genuine panic, I stopped the boat.

I had been warned by an old sea captain, "If you find yourself in shallow water, return to deeper water exactly on your entrance

*Mackinac Island has held a special place in our hearts since our honeymoon. After making a promise to return with our own boat, we fulfilled our dream thirty-three years later.*

path." Rather than try to figure out why we were suddenly in shallow water, I carefully backed into deeper water. Now I had to determine where we were before we could move.

The first order was to change our horn signal to a prolonged blast every two minutes.

I checked the chart and our present location. In an instant, I realized I had made a terrible charting mistake. I had entered the position data for Detour Harbor, not the entrance into the St. Marys River. The harbor was located in town, a couple miles north of the safe entrance into the river. We were heading directly into the rocky shore line of northern Lake Huron, toward downtown Detour.

I quickly plotted the course to the proper entrance of the St. Marys River, and we were underway again. In the next hour, the fog lifted, and we were relieved to find that we were right on the proper course when we sighted the Detour Reef Lighthouse off the bow. Oh, happy day!

*Hessel Harbor marks the entrance to the Thousand Islands.*

From that day forward, I've always double-checked all waypoints to make certain I haven't made a mistake.

We had a celebration in Detour—and I won't repeat what Elaine said to me about our foggy adventure. But we gained experience cruising in fog. I was so proud of Elaine. She continued in the role of first mate for the next seventeen years.

On our return to Lake Erie, we passed Shipwreck Alley and stayed outside of the NORDMEER as we turned to a southerly course. It was late morning and the lake was flat, with hardly a ripple. The FM radio was playing soothing music. Elaine had her head on my shoulder as we skimmed over the water at twenty-five miles per hour. Suddenly I heard a noise growing louder and louder. Fearing some problem with the engine or outdrive, I turned my head to look back. What I saw caused me to hyperventilate.

An A-10 Warthog fighter jet was skimming along close to the surface of the water, coming right at us. Everything was happening

*Flower Pot Island is aptly named, a beautiful sea stack formation that has served as a landmark for countless sailors and boaters through countless centuries.*

so fast. As the fighter came closer and closer, the sound became deafening. Almost on top of us, it suddenly turned to the starboard side of the boat and crossed in front of us with its wing tip appearing to be skipping over the water. The afterburner jet blast sound was a loud BANG! as the plane shot upward and disappeared from view. I glanced up to see his wingman flying straight on the port side.

As I looked back on the formerly flat sea, the wake was all over the surface of the lake and looked like someone had been slalom skiing down a steep hill. My heart was racing, but I quickly pulled myself together. I am certain those pilots told this story the rest of their lives, as I am writing it now.

### THE GEORGIAN BAY CRUISE

As we headed north from Victoria Harbor on the marked channel through the thirty thousand islands of Georgian Bay, I yelled to Elaine down in the galley, "Hon, forget the coffee! We're dead in the water, and I need you NOW!"

She quickly climbed up the steps to the helm. "What's wrong?"

"I've steered us off the channel, and I need you to hold the chart near me so I can figure out what went wrong." I pointed forward at a green can and admitted, "That can should be right here on the starboard side," as I pointed down to the water on that side. "I don't know what's wrong. It's too far ahead. We should be beside it. I can only see underwater rocks in front and starboard."

Elaine was looking to the port side and said, "There's a green can back there," pointing to a can behind our position. As I carefully placed the engines in reverse, I asked Elaine to move to the swim platform and look into the water to see if there were any rocks behind us as I backed up.

"I don't see any," she reported.

After carefully backing into the correct channel, I was able to determine how I missed seeing the green can Elaine pointed out. "I certainly made a mistake," I admitted, as we moved around the can. "I saw the green can straight ahead of the boat, but didn't see this one."

*We headed through a narrow and very tight channel as we entered Georgian Bay.*

Georgian Bay is entirely in Canada and east of the main body of Lake Huron. The only direct water access from Lake Huron is the opening at the northern tip of the Ontario's Bruce Peninsula and the southern end of Ontario's very large Manitoulin Island. Manitoulin Island is the largest freshwater lake island in the world and has one hundred lakes of its own.

The entrance from Lake Huron into Georgian Bay is approximately twelve miles in overall length and filled with many restrictions to limit the access from Lake Huron into the bay. In the center of the entrance is Cove Island. South of the island, two marked channels weave through the rock formations, while two marked and named channels run north of the island. The south channels are the Hurd Channel, located close to the tip of the Bruce Peninsula, and the Devil Channel. Main Channel and the Fitzwilliam Channel are north of the island.

The Hurd Channel is extremely narrow, so the twists and turns require special attention. Any attempt to enter Georgian Bay through the Hurd requires detailed charts and a continuous watch

> "Big Chute Marine Railway is the only marine railway of its kind in North America. Built in 1917, it has been instrumental in keeping sea lamprey from inland Canadian lakes."

for markers. It is easy to see a forward red or green marker and not the same colored marker that is closer to you, as I just described. If you aren't careful, you might find the rock that takes out your drive system.

Georgian Bay, the bay of thirty thousand islands, is 120 miles long and fifty miles wide. It lies in a northwest-to-southeast direction, approximately at a forty-five degree angle from True North. Since it is considered part of Lake Huron, the deepest point is not called out on my charts, but I did find one area where it was five hundred feet deep, right off the northern tip of the Bruce Peninsula. Its average depth is 150 feet, and the surface area is 5,700 square miles. As a result, Georgian Bay represents eleven percent of the defined area of Lake Huron.

The two main river entrances to the bay from the east are the Trent-Severn Waterway (Trent River), in the southeastern corner of the bay, and the French River, on the northeastern end of the bay. Both of these rivers originate in Ottawa, a major city during the 1600s and the capital of Canada today. These rivers represent what I describe as the Interstate 80 for the French and Dutch during the 1600s. Numerous additional rivers feed the Georgian Bay, and a majority of the thirty thousand islands are located on the eastern rocky coast.

The western shore of the bay along the Bruce Peninsula is rock-free, and its depth drops off very quickly from the shoreline all the way to the lower bay area. In contrast, the eastern shore all the way from the south to the north end is lined with islands and rocks, which extend at least five miles out into Georgian Bay. The cruise northward through these thousands of islands and rocks along the eastern shoreline was going to be the new challenge in my plan to become the most experienced and best Great Lakes captain.

Our introduction to cruising Georgian Bay began in 1996 with our 370 Sea Ray Express Cruiser ELEANA, equipped with Raymarine radar, chart plotter, Global Positioning System (GPS), autopilot, compass, VHF, and upgraded depth finder. It had been initiated into our family of ELEANAs in 1995, on our first cruise into Lake Superior, and proved to be a perfect vessel for heavy seas and comfort in port.

We planned a two-week cruise, and we acquired all the charts necessary for this challenge. A couple of our boating friends had visited Tobermory, Ontario, on the northern tip of the Bruce Peninsula, but we weren't able to find anyone who had explored the lower or upper parts of Georgian Bay. This cruise was just what I wanted us to undertake as captain and first mate.

We entered the Hurd Channel and carefully maneuvered through the rocks, constantly comparing the channel markers to our paper chart, even though our computer screen was showing the markers. Our destination was Tobermory, and we were hopeful we could get a dock in Little Tub Marina. Additional dockage was available in Big Tub Marina, but that would require transportation into town. Over our numerous visits to Tobermory, we docked in both marinas.

*The North Channel Lighthouse marks the way for boaters winding their way through one of the 30,000 islands off the eastern shore of Georgian Bay.*

As we neared the tip of the Bruce Peninsula, we spotted the unique and beautiful Flower Pot Island. Farther to the east is tree-covered Bear Rump Island. Flower Pot Island is known for its beautiful sea stack formations of rock, maybe forty or fifty feet high, with trees growing on the top. The base is perhaps twenty feet in diameter, and the top is forty feet in diameter. Awesome!

Slowly entering the channel into Tobermory, we continued south. Luckily, we found a dock right in Tobermory at Little Tub Marina. The quaint town was filled with shops and restaurants, so we stayed for a few nights.

Departing from Tobermory, our goal was to cruise south to Victoria Harbor in Severn Sound, approximately three miles from the termination of the Trent-Severn Waterway. I carefully plotted the 120-mile course down to Hope Island, located just east of Christian Island, where we entered a channel weaving through islands into Severn Sound. When we arrived at Victoria Harbor Marina, newly constructed and with a fantastic staff, they offered a car for us to take a land voyage to visit the Big Chute on Severn.

The Trent-Severn Waterway connects Lake Ontario to Georgian Bay and consists of forty-five locks. It was originally a southern canoeing route the ancients used for thousands of years as a water and portage travel path from Lake Ontario to Georgian Bay and onward into Lake Huron.

Big Chute Marine Railway is the only marine railway of its kind in North America. Built in 1917, it has been instrumental in keeping sea lamprey from inland Canadian lakes.

*The Big Chute Railroad is part of the Trent-Severn Waterway, which consists of forty-five locks leading from Lake Ontario to Georgian Bay. The railroad lowers boats fifty-eight feet into Lock 45. This is the only marine railroad in North America.*

Located after Lock 44 of the forty-five locks of the Trent-Severn Waterway, this rail system lowers pleasure craft fifty-eight feet to Lock 45 or lifts boats from Lock 45 to Lock 44. After boats clear Lock 45, they are on Severn Sound. During our visit, we observed pleasure craft lowered to Lock 45 while another was lifted to Lock 44.

Departing from Victoria Marina, our objective was to follow the marked channel ninety miles north, through the twisting and turning of the channel between the islands. Following the marked narrow channel, we hoped to reach Snug Harbor Marina. But I hadn't make a reservation.

As we slowly maneuvered through the twists and turns around rock islands, we were able to see the bottom in twelve to fifteen feet of extremely clear water. The gorgeous day and breathtaking views caused us to be quite late when we arrived in Parry Sound, not far from Snug Harbor. We decided to find a dock in town and call Snug Harbor to be certain we had a dock for a late arrival. Stopping

> "Sailboats find the North Channel the ideal place to find a cove and tie off to trees and rocks to enjoy the beauty and tranquility, often all alone."

at a store, the owner allowed us to use his phone to call Snug Harbor. To my dismay, we were informed they were fully booked.

The owner of the store recommended we go to Killbear Provincial Park Marina on Killbear Island. Using the store phone, we booked an available dock at Killbear and set off on our way.

What a stroke of luck! This stop was one of the most memorable of all our overnight stays in Georgian Bay.

The Ontario Provincial Park is huge, covering the entire island of Killbear. It is accessible by car and contains defined camp grounds, all overseen by a park ranger. That afternoon, the ranger took the time to show us through the main lodge, which is loaded with information about the park, and described its history as a stop-off point for early travelers and explorers from the 1600s to the 1800s. He recommended trails for us to walk and warned us to be on the lookout for bear and rattlesnakes. "Do not stray off the trails!"

The next day, we decided to explore the park and island. Campers were scattered across the entire huge island. In certain areas, we could hear the rattle of the snakes as we walked by. We came upon an area where campers had set up their tents despite numerous signs warning, RATTLESNAKE CROSSING.

When we returned to the Ranger Station, I asked if many people had been bitten by rattlesnakes. He said he only knew of one man, who was bitten at night as he stepped out of his tent. What a challenging place to camp.

Due to time constraints, this was our last stop on our first cruise in this area. It turned out to be our only venture into the southern and eastern Georgian Bay of Ontario. After two weeks of exploration, we reluctantly headed back to the Lake Huron entrance, knowing we had experienced a part of the Great Lakes that was legendary. This area had been the Interstate 80 of its time, long before the white man arrived.

Our next stop was Mackinac Island, a regular stop whenever we were in northern Lake Huron.

## THE NORTH CHANNEL

Canada's Ontario North Channel stretches from the northwest end of Georgian Bay westward to the St. Marys River. Its southern boundary is Michigan's Drummond Island and Ontario's Cockburn and Manitoulin islands. These three islands form the northern shoreline of Lake Huron.

The North Channel is 160 miles long, and its width is difficult to describe, since the channel is filled with islands. Based on our trips, I would guess the North Channel is ten miles wide at its widest point.

Sailboats find the North Channel the ideal place to find a cove and tie off to trees and rocks to enjoy the beauty and tranquility, often all alone. An ideal destination for pleasure craft, it is narrow and well protected from waves and storms' rough waters. The safe passages through the islands are well marked, and if the captain is alert, finding underwater rocks can be held to a minimum. Unfortunately I have heard of many rock discoveries resulting in costly underwater propeller and shaft replacements.

The main marinas are Meldrum Bay, Gore Bay, Little Current, and Killarney. On our trips, Elaine and I needed to find a marina to dock, as we needed electrical shore power. We never operated our on-board generator, because its noise would destroy the quiet and create the danger of carbon monoxide. In addition, we enjoyed finding restaurants and enjoying a glass of wine as we watched a marvelous sunset.

Our special harbor is Meldrum Bay Marina. For many years, in late mornings. a local lady would arrive in her old station wagon with the rear seats folded down and the entire back covered with delicious baked goods: homemade breads, pies, cakes and cookies. The pies were to "die for."

A commercial fisherman would also arrive in his steel closed-in northern Great Lakes fishing boat and sell fresh caught and cleaned whitefish. I learned from him that whitefish are non-carnivorous, have a small mouth, consume plankton, and must be netted. As a result, Elaine and I have enjoyed whitefish ever since this experience.

One restaurant was located up on a bluff overlooking beautiful Meldrum Bay and marina. I assume in order for the business to survive, they advertised they would prepare a fisherman's whitefish or meat for dinner. They were thus saved from having to invest in costly inventory.

Little Current is near the east end of the North Channel and is the narrowest one-half-mile point between the mainland and Manitoulin Island. While docked for a few days in Little Current, we once were entertained by a family of mink, the parents and three kits living in the channel bank. They played on our assigned dock only a couple feet away from our boat.

In Little Current we discovered a restaurant that almost always featured Arctic Char on the menu, and we looked forward to eating there. The northernmost freshwater fish in the world, Arctic Char thrives in the entire Arctic region and is delicious. The meat is pink

> "Michigan's Saginaw Bay is part of Lake Huron. It is defined by a line drawn from the tip of the thumb of Michigan to Tawas Point on Michigan's east side mainland."

and red, and the taste is similar to trout and salmon. I grew up eating brook, brown, rainbow, and lake trout in Michigan's Upper Peninsula. We certainly enjoyed these dinners and always looked forward to our next visit to Little Current.

The east pleasure craft entrance from Georgian Bay is Killarney, Ontario. This narrow passage has restaurants and services for vacationers, as it is accessible by car, and boaters can find all the services for fuel and maintenance here.

### THE SAGINAW BAY

Michigan's Saginaw Bay is part of Lake Huron. It is defined by a line drawn from the tip of the thumb of Michigan to Tawas Point on Michigan's east side mainland. Michigan's lower peninsula is shaped like a winter mitten with the thumb on the east side.

The bay is approximately fifty miles long and twenty miles at its widest point, and its one thousand square miles represent two percent of the total area of Lake Huron.

*The scenery of Georgian Bay is rugged, often lined by towering rock cliffs.*

*There's nothing better than enjoying the scenery at the end of a beautiful day boating.*

The northern one-third of the bay is the deepest, with depths of one hundred feet, while the depth of the lower two-thirds of the bay average a mere ten to twelve feet. A fifteen-mile shipping channel extends from the Saginaw River to the twenty-five-foot depth area near the north shore of the bay. Most of the lake freighters need at least this depth to navigate and reach the Saginaw River. The bottom of the bay is mainly sand, which makes it ideal for fishing lake perch and walleye.

Since the bay is on the east side of Michigan and protected by the thumb of Michigan, only winds from the northeast create powerful storms. But the most prevalent winds are from the west and north.

## AN AFTER THOUGHT

During our seventeen years of exploring the Great Lakes, we passed through Lake Huron whenever we cruised north to Lake Superior or Lake Michigan. Our experiences on Lake Huron helped prepare us for all of our future travels on the big waters in and surrounding our United States of America. ∎

*At anchor in a scenic marina, we could relax and watch a succession of lakers, freighters, oil tankers, sailboats, and other pleasure craft move across the horizon.*

LAKE HURON, "THE FRESH WATER SEA"

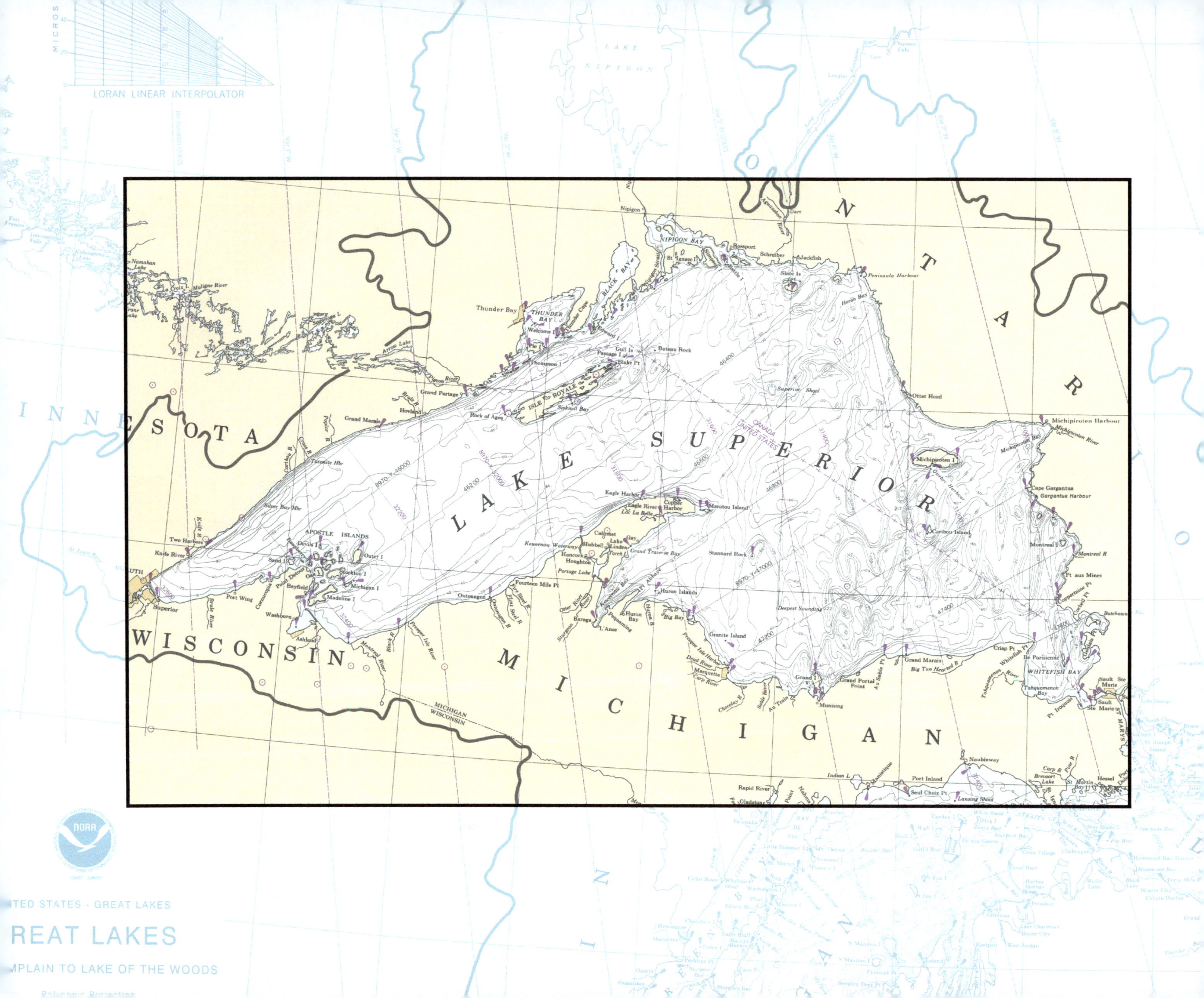
LORAN LINEAR INTERPOLATOR
MICROS
LAKE SUPERIOR
ONTARIO
MINNESOTA
WISCONSIN
MICHIGAN
MICHIGAN WISCONSIN
CANADA UNITED STATES
Nipigon
NIPIGON BAY
Rossport
Schreiber
Jackfish
Slate Is
Peninsula Harbour
Heron Bay
Thunder Bay
THUNDER BAY
Welcome I
BLACK BAY
Pie I
Thompson I
Gull Is
Passage I
Blake Pt
Bateau Rock
Grand Portage
Pigeon River
Arrow Lake
Hovland
Grand Marais
Rock of Ages
ISLE ROYALE
Siskiwit Bay
Superior Shoal
Otter Head
Michipicoten Harbour
Michipicoten River
Michipicoten Bay
Michipicoten I
Cape Gargantua
Gargantua Harbour
Caribou Island
Montreal I
Montreal R
Pt aux Mines
Coppermine Pt
Batchawana Bay
Taconite Hbr
Silver Bay Hbr
Two Harbors
Knife River
Duluth
Superior
Port Wing
APOSTLE ISLANDS
Devils I
Sand I
Outer I
Stockton I
Michigan I
Madeline I
Bayfield
Washburn
Ashland
Ontonagon
Fourteen Mile Pt
Eagle Harbor
Eagle River
Copper Harbor
Lac La Belle
Manitou Island
Keweenaw Waterway
Calumet
Lake Linden
Hubbell
Torch L
Hancock
Houghton
Portage Lake
Gay
Grand Traverse Bay
Stannard Rock
Huron Islands
Huron Bay
Keweenaw Bay
L'Anse
Baraga
Big Bay
Granite Island
Deepest Sounding 222
Presque Isle Harbor
Marquette
Dead River
Carp River
Chocolay R
Grand I
Munising
Au Train
Grand Portal Point
Au Sable Pt
Grand Marais
Big Two Hearted R
Crisp Pt
Whitefish Pt
Ile Parisienne
WHITEFISH BAY
Tahquamenon Bay
Tahquamenon River
Pt Iroquois
Sault Ste Marie
Naubinway
Port Inland
Seul Choix Pt
Lansing Shoal
Manistique
Indian L
Rapid River
Gladstone
Brevoort Lake
St Martin Bay
Hessel
8970-Y-46000
8970-Y-47000
UNITED STATES - GREAT LAKES
GREAT LAKES
CHAMPLAIN TO LAKE OF THE WOODS
Polyconic Projection

# CHAPTER 6
# Lake Superior: Big Sea Waters

**THE BIG SEA LADY** gave us Her first challenge even before we had eaten our lunch.

While we approached Whitefish Point, the land and the lake were suddenly covered with a vertical wall of solid fog as far up as we could see. The Upper Peninsula's Whitefish Point projects into Lake Superior, forcing all inbound and outbound vessels to go around it in order to enter into the lake or leave the lake and return to the Soo Locks.

On this particular day, we were taken by surprise when we were confronted with a thick fog, because we had been enjoying a beautiful, sunny, cloudless day when we departed from Ontario's Roberta Bondar Marina and passed through the MacArthur Lock into Lake Superior. I had never seen or been confronted by this strange fog. The Big Sea Lady had prepared a totally new challenge for us.

### LAKE SUPERIOR VISITS
#### DESTINATION ONTONAGON

Our Great Lakes adventures began by exploring Lake Erie and Lake Huron in our 290 Sea Ray Sundancer during the summers of 1992, 1993, and 1994. In the summer of 1995, we decided to take the next big step in our adventures by exploring Lake Superior on our new (to us) 1994 370 Sea Ray Express Cruiser, which was fitted with the latest technology: RAYMARINE radar, chart plotter, Global Positioning System (GPS), autopilot, compass, VHF, and upgraded depth finder.

This boat was forty feet long and twelve feet wide. Its full galley featured a microwave, refrigerator, two-burner stove, sink, plenty of cupboards, and seating for six at the dining table. The table and seating also could be made into a bed. It had one complete head with shower and a forward state room.

This ELEANA was powered by a 120-volt generator, which would supply electrical power while underway to the 120-volt utilities, refrigerator, and heating or air conditioning in the lower living area. In addition, 120-volt shore power, vac-u-flush head, seventy gallons of fresh water, twenty-eight gallons of sewage, 350 gallons of gasoline, and twin V8 inboards made this boat ideal for cruising on all the Great Lakes.

We selected the last two weeks of July and first week of August 1995 for this undertaking, and we shared our plan with Dick and Dorothy, friends from the Midwest who were experienced Lake Erie boaters. They were enthusiastic about visiting more of the Great Lakes with us, but had only two weeks of vacation time.

I laid out a plan that included overnight stops on Lake Huron and Lake Superior. The main target was to spend one week of their two weeks on Lake Superior. They made plans to fly home from Hancock, Michigan, which would provide an additional week for Elaine and me to make our first on-water visit to Ontonagon from Lake Superior.

The overnight stop at Sault Saint Marie was planned with options and allowances for bad weather. At the Soo (Sault Saint Marie's nickname) we would go through what is affectionately called

*Named for General Douglas MacArthur, the MacArthur Lock at Sault St. Marie lowers and raises boats twenty-five feet as they travel between Lake Huron and Lake Superior.*

the "Linchpin of the Great Lakes," locks that link the lower Great Lakes to Lake Superior. Built in 1855, they are operated and maintained by the U.S. Army Corps of Engineers.

The MacArthur Lock, named after General Douglas MacArthur, is mainly used by pleasure craft and freighters while the Poe Lock is frequently used by iron ore and grain freighters. The locks raise and lower vessels the twenty-five feet between Lake Superior and Lakes Huron and Michigan. These locks don't use pumps to raise and lower vessels, only Lake Superior water, another way the Big Sea Lady demonstrates Her power. In addition, Her water carries ninety-five percent of the entire iron ore mined in the United States.

Upon arrival at the Soo, we stayed overnight at Ontario's Roberta Bondar Marina. Early the next morning, we were directed by U.S. Army Corps Soo Lock Control to enter the MacArthur Lock for our first lift and entrance into Lake Superior. I still recall those special and fearful feelings as we exited into the Big Sea Water and wondered what She had in mind for our next two weeks. We soon found the first challenge.

We continued on the St Marys River until we entered into Whitefish Bay in clear and bright sunshine with only a slight summer breeze. But facing us was a wall of solid fog.

I stopped the boat in the sunlight and pondered how we should proceed. Since ELEANA was fitted with radar, I turned it on and began adjusting settings. Studying the screen, I set the distance so the entire Whitefish Point was visible, and then observed a moving spot on the screen indicating a freighter was coming around the point. Not wanting to be in the fog at the same time, we moved well out of the way with the intent of letting the freighter pass before we entered. I wondered how far we would have to cruise in the fog.

We were being challenged with advection fog, which suddenly forms when warm, moist air moves off the land over the lake's cold water. The air is quickly cooled to saturation by the cold water below, and a thick vertical fog forms over a large area. What else did the Big Sea Lady have in store for us before we even entered Her?

I can't adequately describe the sensation of passing into a solid wall of very thick fog. It is as if a door closes behind us and we are suddenly alone in the hands of the Big Sea Lady. To me, She was saying to the moist air, "Don't you dare come over my cold water."

Enshrouded in white, we slowly rounded Whitefish Point, managing to stay closer to shore and away from the possibility of any other downbound Laker. As suddenly as the fog wall had closed around the boat in Whitefish Bay, we unexpectedly exited into bright, clear sunlight, a reminder that the Big Sea Lady had many surprises in her depths— and, of course, She wasn't finished with us.

We sped along at twenty-five miles per hour on a nearly flat surface, aiming for the Pictured Rocks National Park shoreline, thirteen miles of colorful sandstone rock formations towering up to two hundred feet above Lake Superior. When the sandstone ages

*Every time we returned to Mackinac Island, Elaine and I visited our very special bench.*

and falls off the cliffs, new colors and shapes of caves and castle turrets appear. God's creation and majesty displayed.

We expected to arrive around noon and dock in Munising Marina. Elaine and I knew of a bar that sold homemade pasties (the Upper Peninsula's famous Finnish meal wrapped in a pastry shell), and we needed to buy them for our dinner before they sold out.

Well, it didn't take very long for the Big Sea Lady to arrange for a surprise. I needed to go below, so I asked Elaine to take the helm and maintain the heading set on the chart plotter. As soon as I left, BANG! I immediately knew we had hit a deadhead and rushed topside.

Elaine had expertly placed the drives in neutral and brought the engines to idle. Our friends were pointing at a floating deadhead log

LAKE SUPERIOR—BIG SEA WATERS

*Elaine displays her "deadhead trophy"—a damaged propeller that was fixed by a local Upper Peninsula craftsman, to our great relief.*

with a new, very deep, curved design along its length. I quickly opened the engine hatch cover to check for water entry. Seeing none, I went into the galley and opened the floor boards to check for water, since I had heard the log slam into the hull right under my feet. Seeing none, I returned to breathing.

Over the years, I heard experienced old-time captains often say, "Deadheads on the Great Lakes normally stay within five miles of shore." I never heard why, but always assumed it had to be due to currents, changing water depths, and shore wave actions.

I had set a course for the entrance into Munising Harbor between Pictured Rocks and Grand Island that gradually brought us less than five miles from shore. I normally kept the boat outside the five-mile goal, but on this day, I hadn't followed my rule. Perhaps the Big Lady wanted us to slow down and take in Her gorgeous shoreline. Was She in control?

Letting out a huge breath, I took the helm and checked the port and starboard props by placing them individually in forward and reverse. Both props moved the boat, but the starboard prop vibrated, which meant it needed replacement. I always carried spare props, so I wasn't worried. But I knew the boat had to be lifted out of the water to check the hull and replace the propeller.

I rechecked for water entry on the starboard propeller shaft in the engine compartment. Not finding any water intrusion, I used only the port propeller to move us slowly past Pictured Rocks.

When we approached the marina, I called and requested dockage and assistance, since only one propeller might make docking difficult. Two men were waiting, and docking was uneventful. The harbormaster assisted, and after tying off the boat, I told him of our problem. Immediately he said, "The owner of the boat lift for the Glass Bottom Tour Boats is in my office right now. I'll ask him to come and talk to you."

Dick Morrison walked down to our boat, and I gave him a summary of what happened. In the course of discussions, I asked if he knew Bill Perttula, a distant relative who lived in town on M-28. "Of course I know Bill."

He continued, "I can lift your boat right now. Bring it over to the lift. You can see it over there." He pointed to the western shoreline. "Let's take care of this right away."

We untied ELEANA and motored over to the lift area. When we arrived, Dick had already lowered the lift slings into the water, and I drove right into them.

I removed the starboard propeller from the boat's engine compartment and exited the boat, as the slings were already lifting ELEANA out of the water. While Dick was removing and installing the new prop, I checked the hull for damage. I could only find a small scratch in the bottom paint.

> "The next morning started with bright sun and seas of one-to-two feet. Our destination was Marquette."

We asked Elaine to hold her trophy, the damaged propeller, and Dorothy took a picture of us. I wondered if I would have to sleep topside that night, but she took the ribbing with her usual grace. All operations for correcting the deadhead problem were completed in less than two hours. It was time to thank the Lord and celebrate.

We walked to the bar, played pool, had drinks, and sat down to eat the pasties we so coveted. Later, sitting on the aft area of ELEANA, we reviewed the events of the day and marveled at the way we had avoided a catastrophe. How fortunate we were to be on Lake Superior! The Lady had given us a real scare, but at the end of the day, all was wonderful.

The next morning started with bright sun and seas of one-to-two feet. Our destination was Marquette, approximately forty-five miles, which would take us two hours while cruising at our normal speed. Clearing the marina, we were forced to control our wake for about two miles before increasing to cruising speed. Upon synchronizing the port and starboard engines to the normal 3,000 rpm, the boat began turning to the starboard direction rather than going straight. I had to increase the starboard rpm to 3300 in order to cruise in a straight direction.

What happened? What did the Lady do overnight?

Well, it was quite easy for me to figure out why this happened. When I purchased the spare propellers, I specified "cupped" propellers. Cupping a propeller increases the boat speed by ten percent when operating at the same rpm. The new spare props weren't cupped, since they are always cupped in matched pairs. Visually it is almost impossible to see if a propeller is cupped. This was definitely my problem. I had not confirmed whether they were cupped when I purchased them. Live and learn.

I certainly wasn't going to continue to operate the boat with a 300 rpm difference between port and starboard for the next two weeks. I had to get this new propeller cupped, but to have this done in the Upper Peninsula was going to require a miracle. Holding my hands over my face, I thought, "What am I going to do? Why now?"

Our ride to Marquette was quiet and uneventful, since everyone knew how upset I was. Upon arrival in Marquette, I chose to dock at the Lower Harbor because we would be downtown. An end T-dock was assigned to us because the Lower Harbor docks were constructed for thirty-foot boats, and ours was forty feet.

Elaine had called my sister Tricia as we approached Marquette, and she was there to greet us. After the introductions and getting caught up with the boat situation, Tricia said, "I have a friend who keeps his large boat in the Upper Harbor. I'm sure he can help with your problem. I'm going to call him."

After checking in with the harbormaster, we walked up the hill to the Vierling Restaurant to have lunch. I was ready for a bowl of their famous whitefish soup. During lunch, Tricia's friend called and said he would meet us at the harbor at two o'clock.

When Ed arrived, I explained the cupped propeller problem and our situation. "There is no one around here who can cup props, so let's look at the damaged prop and determine if it can be fixed," he suggested. When I retrieved it from ELEANA, Ed looked it over and told us of a young local man in town who repairs propellers for the Department of Natural Resources. "I'll bet he can bend it back to its original shape."

I was surprised and hoped this might be a solution, but the Lower Harbor didn't have a boat lift. Ed saw the look on my face, and continued, "Jeff, my son, is a diver. I know he can change the prop

# "We were unable to see through the fog. I felt overpowering fear set in. Fortunately no wind existed, and I turned on the radar."

here in the marina after the prop is repaired. No problem. In fact he is at home. He will come and take you to have the prop repaired." He called the prop repairman, who said that he was free and would be willing to do it right away—in fact, we could even wait for it.

The repairman lived in Harvey, a few miles away, and Jeff and I were there in about twenty minutes. A young man in his mid-thirties led us into his garage. On his workbench, he inspected the prop, then took a sledgehammer and slammed it on the blades a couple of times. He placed the prop on a spindle, then onto hand-built "V" blocks to spin the prop. Removing it, he slammed the blades a few more times and repeated the process. On the third check, he said, "Good as new," and handed it to me.

I will admit I wasn't ready. I knew how sensitive and critical the balance and shape had to be to avoid vibrations. "What do I owe you?"

"Twenty bucks."

With my mouth probably open, I paid him and offered a "Thank you."

Back at the marina, Jeff donned his diving gear, tied his wrenches to his wetsuit, and proceeded to disappear under the boat to remove the non-cupped prop and install the reworked original.

"We'll stick around for you to check it out," Ed told me.

Heading out beyond the breakwater wall so I could create boat wake, I sped up to maximum speed. To my amazement, there was no vibration, and perfect synchronization of engines. Amazing!

I am always so thankful to the Lord for His way of placing people in front of us when we face a need—again.

I invited Ed on board to celebrate, but he and Jeff had more things to do. So in the spirit of celebration, Tricia, Elaine, Dick, Dorothy, and I opened a bottle of wine and saluted Elaine for giving up her trophy so we could continue our voyage on Lake Superior.

As I reflect back on those last couple of days, I believe the Big Sea Lady placed that deadhead and caused all this chaos knowing that a drama plus U.P. people and family would make this an exciting cruise.

What else does She have in store for us? I wondered.

After enjoying Marquette for a couple of days, we departed for Copper Harbor on the tip of the Keweenaw Peninsula. Copper Harbor is the northern end of U.S. Route 41, and Miami, Florida is two thousand miles to the southern end of Route 41.

That day the lake seas were two to four feet, so we had a bumpy ride during the first hour, but the wind died and the seas dropped to one to two feet the rest of the way. Passing between the peninsula and Manitou Island, we turned west and headed for the green can marking the entrance to Copper Harbor.

Arriving around noon, we saw the green can clearly visible from a mile away, but the south shoreline was not. Another advection fog totally obscured the entire peninsula.

We were unable to see through the fog. I felt overpowering fear set in. Fortunately no wind existed, and I turned on the radar. From our position near the green can, the radar barely outlined the narrow entrance.

Looking at the chart, the entrance from the green can was defined by a True 181-degree entry to a rock wall, and then a ninety

*We're standing in Copper Harbor, at the head of U.S. Route 41. As the sign shows, the road ends in Miami, Florida, 1,990 miles away.*

degree turn to starboard. The marina was a quarter of a mile on the direct path from the ninety-degree turn. I wondered if we could find a dock once we were in the marina area. I guessed the Big Lady had been easing us into what She really can create.

The chart indicated we were located on the surface of the earth where the compass correction factor of True to Magnetic was minus four degrees, so we needed to enter at 177 degrees on the compass heading. In addition, the radar might show the rocks on each side of the entrance.

Fortunately, the Lady was totally calm as we approached, and I was grateful that we didn't have waves of any size to create a more serious challenge entering into the thick fog. As we slowly proceeded into the abyss, once again the fog door closed behind us. I could barely see the boat's bow pulpit, and entry rock walls were barely visible on the radar screen. Suddenly, the forward view was solid red. The huge bright red range marker loomed through the fog, making me think we were going to crash into it. I immediately stopped, using a strong reverse.

*A stunning sunset was the reward after a tense, fog-bound adventure.*

We now had to make the ninety-degree turn to starboard. As we turned and slowly moved in the westerly direction, the radar suddenly indicated a boat coming directly at us. My reaction was to turn to starboard, but rocks were visible on the radar, so I stopped at about the same time as the small aluminum boat coming at us. The captain was obviously stunned to see a huge boat in front of him. He veered off to his starboard side. Elaine said she saw the surprised look on his face as he looked up at our bow, which probably towered ten feet above him. He averted a collision and then stopped.

As we continued slowly through the fog, we abruptly found ourselves in bright sunlight with no clouds, while the wall of fog lingered behind us. We were so thankful to the Lord for our safe arrival. We were the only boat at the marina.

Later, after a wonderful dinner prepared on one of the marina's charcoal fire stands, we opened a bottle of wine and sat on the aft seating area of ELEANA, marveling at the gorgeous sunset.

The following morning dawned clear and bright, and revealed a sailboat on its side in the rocks near the entrance. The Big Sea

# "The twenty-two-mile Keweenaw Waterway was completed in 1874, the key for providing access to the copper needed for American industry."

Lady had evidently accomplished Her goal of showing Her power and control of Her water to another captain and crew. It could well have been us.

Since I had visited the area many times in my youth, and Elaine and I had vacationed there a couple of times, we spent the day touring the area with Dick and Dorothy, using the harbor's courtesy car. After a drive through historic Fort Wilkins State Park, Brockway Mountain Drive, and shopping, we finished the day with a fantastic dinner on a restaurant deck overlooking the harbor and Lake Superior.

Fort Wilkins was built in 1844, when copper exploration and mining were attracting many miners and families into the area. When the indigenous people (Ojibwa) objected to the intrusion into their tribal land, a treaty was established that gave non-indigenous people the right to search and mine for copper. The fort was closed and sold in 1855, shortly after the area became part of the State of Michigan.

The next day we departed for the man-made, twenty-two-mile-long Keweenaw Waterway. Natural rivers flowing from Portage Lake westward into Lake Superior and eastward into Keweenaw Bay originally separated the Keweenaw Peninsula from the Upper Peninsula of Michigan. In past times, this upper area was called Copper Island, since it contained so much solid copper and copper ore.

The indigenous people used this natural waterway to traverse the peninsula. Portage and Torch lakes are close together and located more on the eastern side of the peninsula. Portage Lake is fed by the Sturgeon River, which flows from the south. Torch Lake is fed by the Trap Rock River from the north, and its outflow goes to Portage Lake. Two rivers flow out of Portage Lake, one heading west to Lake Superior, and a smaller and shallower one flowing east to Keweenaw Bay.

The discovery of copper in the area and the resulting mining boom meant the transportation of goods into, and copper out of, this area had to be improved. Rail wasn't going to be the answer, so water was the natural solution.

In the 1860s, the deepest river flowing west to Lake Superior was dredged to a depth of twenty-five feet, providing freighters with access from Lake Superior all the way to Portage Lake.

The canal joining Portage Lake and Torch Lake was also dredged. The Portage River was too small and shallow to accept large vessels, so it was dredged to about twelve feet. Today, pleasure craft use it to cut across the peninsula, thereby saving the one-hundred-mile trip around the north shore of the peninsula.

The twenty-two-mile Keweenaw Waterway was completed in 1874, the key for providing access to the copper needed for American industry.

Two boom towns resulted: Hancock, platted in 1859 on the north shore of the waterway, and Houghton, platted in 1854 on the south shore. They flourished. The copper mines on Copper Island required thousands of miners and support personnel. As a result, new towns were established, often based on ethnic origins. Cornish immigrants arriving from England brought mining skills needed for establishing and operating mines. Other Europeans, particularly Finns, Swedes, and Italians, performed the labor. Calumet was established, and according to the 1900 census, the city had almost five thousand people, and the surrounding townships nearly twenty-five thousand residents. In the census of 2021, Calumet had six hundred ninety-four people. The copper boom had ended long since.

Leaving Copper Harbor, we encountered two-to-three-foot seas for the sixty-mile cruise along the Keweenaw Peninsula. In two and a half hours, we reached the entrance of the 1860s Portage Canal, now called Keweenaw Waterway. The only highway bridge to Copper Island from Michigan crosses the waterway west of Hancock and Houghton. In 1995, it was a swing bridge, and we had to wait for the car and truck traffic to clear before the bridge could swing open for ships taking passengers to Isle Royale. Today, it is a lift bridge, raising the entire four traffic lanes high enough for large ships to enter and exit at the same time.

Finally docking at the Hancock Marina, we had a full day to discover Hancock. Dick and Dorothy confirmed their very early flight and made arrangements for transportation to the airport.

As soon as Dick and Dorothy left, we departed for Ontonagon, our main reason for this trip. It is only forty miles south of the waterway. I was returning to my hometown. During our visit, the town would be celebrating a three-day All Class High School Reunion. Elaine and I previously attended my reunions, but this was the opportunity to meet friends from classes before and after my graduation. This was also my ego trip, as we were the only ones to arrive by boat.

Ontonagon lies on the south shore of Lake Superior, and the Ontonagon River passes through town before it enters the lake. This river is formed from three main branches, East Branch, Middle Branch, and West Branch, all of which originate about fifty miles south of Ontonagon. The town and river are famous for the Ontonagon Boulder, originally located twenty miles upriver from Ontonagon on the West Branch. This huge boulder is believed to have been deposited there by a glacier and was known to our earliest indigenous people, who removed pieces of copper and used them to worship Gitche Manitou, the Great Spirit.

The solid copper boulder weighs 3,708 pounds. Historians believe a Jesuit missionary was the first European to marvel at the rock in 1667. After the 1826 Treaty of Fond du Lac, the Ojibwa gave the U.S. mineral rights to the northern area, including the Upper Peninsula. The rock was then removed and owned by private individuals until the War Department took it over in 1847. In 1860, it was placed in the Smithsonian Museum, where it rests today. A group from Ontonagon continues efforts to have the boulder returned to Ontonagon.

Ontonagon is the first safe harbor east of the Apostle Islands in Wisconsin. In the 1800s, it boomed, shipping copper and lumber out and bringing supplies in.

I immediately began reliving my memory of entering the harbor entrance fifty years earlier when I saw the breakwall projecting out into the lake. As we moved closer, I imagined the waves and the water spray from those huge waves slamming into the rocks. I decided to go farther south, so I could reenact our entry from the west. Our ELEANA was about the same overall length as the charter fishing boat, but I sat four or five feet higher at the helm, so it was hard to imagine being so much closer to the water, as we had been when we entered the harbor on that frightful day. Elaine was asking many questions, as she had only heard me tell the story. I tried to simulate our entry with the day's two-foot waves.

Once inside the breakwall, my mind's eye was searching for the dock and previous location of the charter boat on the north wall, but with the numerous changes, I could only imagine the short slip where we boarded.

I looked upstream at the same old M-64 swing bridge and bridge tender in his booth on the bridge. I called for passage and heard the same horn sound that I had heard fifty years earlier, in the days when I was walking to my girlfriend's house. It continues to warn pedestrians, cars, and trucks that the bridge is preparing to open.

*The same old M-64 swing bridge welcomed us to my hometown, on my first voyage there since 1949.*

As the bridge cleared of traffic and the barriers were lowered, the bridge began to pivot, opening the port side for outbound vessels and the starboard side for our inbound travel. I drove the boat forward very slowly, as my old memories raced through my mind. This was my first entrance into the Ontonagon River since returning in the storm of 1949.

Clearing the bridge, I turned to starboard and into the recently upgraded harbor. The harbormaster assigned a dock by VHF, and we docked and tied off. After registering, we walked across the swing bridge, crossed River Street, and entered Sly's Cafe for lunch.

After celebrating old times for three days with high school friends and relatives, we headed home. To save approximately one hundred miles, we crossed through the Keweenaw Waterway and into Keweenaw Bay. Cruising north out of the bay, we entered into Lake Superior, and encountered four-to-six-foot seas. We had a very rough ride as we cruised around the Huron Mountains, which are the highest natural elevation point in the Upper Peninsula, at 1,979 feet. Finally reaching Marquette, we docked in the Upper Harbor. Departing the next day, we would have a straight eastward path to the deepest spot on Lake Superior and then on to the Soo.

We had studied the charts and knew that the lake's deepest spot was north and east of Grand Island, which protects the Munising Harbor. Amazingly, here Lake Superior has an area only 120 feet deep, while only a couple of miles away, Her lake bottom drops off

*As we approached the swing bridge, the same horn sounded that I had first heard fifty years earlier.*

to a maximum depth of 1,333 feet. It is hard for me to visualize the concept of standing on land and then in a short distance looking down more than one thousand feet to the bottom of a gorge.

The next day, we departed at six o'clock in the morning on our seven-hour, 120-mile cruise to the Soo, with a brief stop planned on the deepest point of Lake Superior. The seas were calm and no wind was blowing, so we comfortably cruised at our synchronized 3,000 rpm.

A depth sounder sends a high frequency signal downward, and when it is is returned after hitting bottom, the signal is converted into a display showing the depth at that point. If the boat glides across the water too fast for the return signal to reach the sounder, the display shows zero. Sounder technology has improved, but in our vessel, deeper water readings were a function of our speed across the water.

At that time, our onboard depth technology couldn't determine when we were on the 1,333 foot point, even if we stopped on the water. The output signal was not powerful enough to travel down the quarter of a mile of water and bounce back to the sounder. To assume we were on location, we first found the 120-foot area by using our onboard depth finder. The chart indicated the direction and distance to the deepest point, and we moved to the location defined by the chart and GPS. The grand Lady was calm that day, and we gave thanks to the Lord for allowing us this unique opportunity.

The afternoon return to the Soo was smooth. Upon entering the lock area, we were directed immediately to enter the Poe Lock. The gates closed behind us. After we were lowered to the St Marys River, we exited and slipped by a lake freighter beginning to enter the Poe Lock. Soon it would be lifted the twenty-five feet and enter into the Big Sea waters.

We called Ontario's Roberta Bondar Marina and were directed to a dock. Since we had a few extra days, we decided to make Mackinac Island our next stop.

We had no idea we were creating another opportunity for a harrowing experience on the Great Lakes.

The next day, we traveled to St. Ignace and stayed overnight. After entering Mackinac Island Harbor the next day, we enjoyed a beautiful day and dinner at the Iroquois Hotel, our favorite restaurant.

We decided to leave early the following morning, but we woke up to very heavy fog. As we pulled out of the harbor to cross the laker shipping lane, the fume alarm went off in the engine compartment, followed by a sudden explosion. I believed I saw smoke in the aft area and yelled "Fire!"

I immediately shut down both engines, while Elaine pulled the fire extinguisher from the helm. As I opened the door in the aft floor, steam poured out. I didn't smell smoke, but water was everywhere, and the bilge pumps were running.

Elaine screamed, "Are we sinking?"

My mind was racing, trying to make sense of what had just happened. At the same time, I realized we were dead in the water in the narrow shipping lane between Bois Blanc and Mackinac Island. "We have to move!" I yelled to Elaine. "Life jacket on!"

I dropped down into the engine compartment and immediately found the port engine's eight-inch exhaust and water-cooling hose had disconnected from the engine. I yelled reassuringly, "We're not sinking!"

To keep the engine cool, lake water is pumped into the engine, and it exits into the eight-inch tube to combine with the engine's exhaust. Both exit from the boat through an underwater exhaust port.

"The starboard engine is okay!" I reported to Elaine, "Start the starboard and move us out of the shipping channel." Then I crawled out of the engine compartment.

Elaine did as I asked. Realizing we were safe and out of the way of danger, we sat together for a moment catching our breath and praying, "Thank you, Lord, for keeping us safe." I know both of us were recalling the image of huge eight-hundred-foot lake freighters passing by the Mackinac Island Harbor, totally silent and not even producing a wake. Followed by a mental picture of what could have happened.

As we sat well out of the channel in calm, thick fog, I was able to get the stiff heavy hose back onto the engine. Only one clamp was intact, since one was broken. I was able to tighten the clamp, and it held the exhaust tube in place.

My farm days must have caused me to include a coil of heavy wire in my stash of emergency items. Using a large screw driver, I was able to tighten coils of wires to replace the broken clamp. After safely arriving home, I replaced the wires and added extra clamps to reinforce the connections on both engines.

This three-week cruise again proved the Big Sea Lady was active in creating extreme adventures for travel on Her waters. However, we were able to overcome all of them. The challenges we encountered were very beneficial in my quest to be the best captain on fresh water.

## DESTINATION ISLE ROYAL

Four years after our previous trip to the Big Sea Lady, in the summer of 1999, we decided to take the 1994 370 Sea Ray Express Cruiser to Isle Royale, which is located in the northwestern basin of Lake Superior.

Our cruise to the St. Marys River included a couple of days on Mackinac Island before passing through the MacArthur Lock into the Big Sea Lady. Our routine stops in Munising, Marquette, and Copper Harbor were problem-free. In Copper Harbor, our stay was delayed due to storms, but the weather forecast changed, and we departed for Isle Royale on the third day.

Located in the northwestern part of Lake Superior, Isle Royale became part of America when the border between America and Canada was first delineated. It also was part of the nine thousand square miles of land given by the Continental government to the Michigan Territory in 1843, to avoid the Toledo War. The 400 islands of Isle Royale became part of the State of Michigan in 1847, and Isle Royale became a township within Houghton County.

In 1861, Houghton County was reduced in size, when Keweenaw County was establish by the Michigan Legislature. Isle Royale then became part of Keweenaw County, and Eagle Harbor, on the Keweenaw Peninsula, was named the county seat.

Isle Royale is the fourth-largest lake island in the world. Uninhabited, it offers visitors pristine wilderness adventures. Native peoples used it as a hunting ground and source of copper for thousands of years. The island was designated a National Park in October, 1940. Its main island is 206 square miles, forty-five miles long, and nine miles wide, surrounded by more than four hundred additional islands. Isle Royale is fifteen miles from Canada, sixty miles from the Keweenaw Peninsula, and 107 miles from Houghton City.

In ancient times, the waters of Lake Superior were considerably colder, and the lake would freeze, creating a pathway for moose, wolves, and small game to reach the island. Now totally isolated, the balance between moose and wolves has been monitored for decades. Wolves' main sources of food are rabbits and beaver.

The park has always maintained strict policies for human visitors, and these rules often change. Before our arrival, I studied the boater rules and regulations for 1999. At that time, Rock Harbor provided docks on a first-come basis. There were no signs indicating no-wake areas, since wake is prohibited in all waters within the boundary.

Most significant for boaters, gray water is never permitted to be discharged from their boats. Gray water is defined as any liquids, but most generally it is the water from the boat's kitchen and bathroom sinks and showers.

So, for us, while we visited the park, we used no soap for any purpose. We rinsed our dishes on land.

Today, the park is concerned about invasive species being brought into the local island waters. Procedures regulate what should be done before a boat enters the park's perimeter waters. My understanding is that dropping an anchor is no longer permitted, as the bottom will be disturbed and release contaminants.

Upon arrival, we found an open dock in Rock Harbor, immediately observing the beauty of the park. We had an opportunity to watch a film explaining what we were permitted to do and safety issues with animals.

During our first night, I awoke to a noise. I went silently topside to see what was happening. A park ranger with a flashlight was checking the water around each boat to determine if there was a sheen from soap or grease discharge. The park means what it says!

We departed Isle Royale with four-to-six-foot seas running abeam, so the boat was rolling side to side, but we safely arrived in Ontonagon. From there, we returned home to Lake Erie.

## OUR LAST CRUISE TO LAKE SUPERIOR

In October of 1999, we sold our well-used 1994 370 Sea Ray Express Cruiser and purchased the larger 1998 400 Sea Ray with twin Caterpillar 3116 diesel engines. The new ELEANA was forty-four feet in overall length, with a fourteen-foot beam. Two staterooms, two heads, a full-size refrigerator, microwave, three-burner electric stove, and plenty of cupboard space made this vessel very comfortable.

This boat had a cruising speed of twenty-seven knots, or thirty miles per hour, held 350 gallons of diesel fuel, and one hundred gallons of fresh water. I fitted it with the latest electronic navigation available, so we were now able to cruise through rougher seas and bad weather.

In 2000, we decided to make what became our final trip to Lake Superior. The first leg was to go to Marquette and pick up my sister Trish. We planned to cruise around the Keweenaw Peninsula, stopping at Copper Harbor and then Hancock on the Keweenaw Waterway. My sister was going to return to Marquette via land yacht, and my brother Joe and sister-in-law Elaine were flying to Hancock from Washington State. Together, we would explore the western shore of the Big Lady.

Upon arriving at Isle Royale, due to the size of ELEANA, no dockage was possible in Rock Harbor. The ranger directed us to a designated location where we were authorized to drop anchor. We had our motorized dinghy on board, so we were able to explore the eastern and north areas around the main island. For two days, we

# "Over our three trips to the Big Sea Lady, Elaine and I circumnavigated 64% of Her shore line."

visited the remote islands and were fascinated by the serene and untouched landscape we saw from the water. We also walked on some of the trails on the east side of the island.

On the third day, we moved down to the western end of the island and entered Washington Bay. After a short stay in Windigo, Isle Royale, for shopping and lunch, we departed for the western coast of Superior.

On the way, we stopped to look at the S.S. AMERICA, a 1928 shipwreck. On a fateful day in June of that year, the S.S. AMERICA sailed out of Duluth on its normal route up the north shore of Lake Superior, to drop passengers off in Windigo. On the return trip, the captain turned the helm over to the first mate and left the bridge. The first mate attempted to navigate the narrows between Thompson Island and the northeastern tip of Isle Royale Island, but crashed into rocks on the starboard side. The single-layered hull was breached. In an attempt to save the ship, the first mate then ran the bow up on the rocks, where it rests today. We could see the rusted vessel above the water and the rear still visible in the lake's cold, clear water. Another sinking attributed to the Big Lady.

Joe and Elaine didn't have their U.S. passports, so we were unable to visit Thunder Bay, Ontario. Instead, we cruised to Grand Marais, Minnesota. No dockage was available, so we dropped anchor in the bay and used the dinghy to explore the harbor. We had a wonderful dinner in Grand Marais.

The next day we saw the mountains of the Mesabi Iron Range from the lake as we entered Duluth Harbor. We had made reservations for two nights at Barker's Island Marina in Superior, Wisconsin. The famous iron-ore loading docks in the Duluth Harbor and on the St. Louis River were fascinating and rugged. Numerous old docks remain dressed in their red finery of iron ore dust.

Duluth is the world's farthest inland port accommodating oceangoing ships, and the busiest port on the Great Lakes. The twin harbors of Duluth and Superior have been the center for shipbuilding since the late 1800s. During World War II, many military ships were built here, including some of the thousand-foot ore carriers that only traverse the Great Lakes, since the Welland Canal can only handle ships up to 766 feet long and eighty feet wide.

After departing out of Superior's harbor into Lake Superior, our next stops were the Apostle Islands and the harbor of Bayfield. These picturesque islands with coves and tunnels are lined with noteworthy homes and cottages. Bayfield is a favorite vacation destination. We found dockage available at Bayfield Marina, and our dinner that evening at St. James Hotel was outstanding.

Departing the next day, we cruised around the Apostle Islands, admiring the terrain and homes before heading for Ontonagon. On the way, we could observe the Porcupine Mountains from the lake. We stopped and relived our former times in the these mountains. Joe was raised in White Pine, the copper-mining town eight miles south of the mountains, and this was my home area in the late 1950s.

After a stop in Ontonagon, the first port of refuge east of Bayfield, we returned to Hancock.

Over the years, Elaine and I made three trips onto the Big Sea Lady. Her shoreline stretches for approximately 1,729 miles. Using an official lake chart and calipers, I estimated that circumnavigating the lake by boat would be approximately 1,100 miles. Using the same method, we cruised close to seven hundred miles, or sixty-four percent of Her vast shores. The Big Sea Lady accepted us and even caused us some scary moments, but I will always remain respectful of Her.

She baptized me in Her waters years ago, and I still get those shivers up my spine when I am near Her. Maybe it's my love and respect! ■

"My sister, Patricia I. Winton, photographed the Big Sea Lady's power on a November day at Black Rock Cove in Marquette, Michigan."

*"Gitche Gumee was photographed at sunrise, when my sister Patricia caught the Big Sea Lady issuing a dire warning to captains."*

LAKE SUPERIOR—BIG SEA WATERS

# CHAPTER 7
# Lake Michigan Summers

**ALTHOUGH ELAINE AND I** are native Michiganders, Lake Michigan wasn't on our normal path of water travel from Lake Erie. However, we did explore the lake and visit as many of its harbors, cities, towns, and marinas as we could. Our favorite harbors were Sheboygan, Fish Creek, and Sister Bay, in Wisconsin, as well as Horseshoe Hammond Casino and B&E Marine in Indiana. We journeyed to Escanaba in the Upper Peninsula to visit my sister, and Muskegon in the lower peninsula to visit another sister and brother-in-law. Frankfort, Northport, Harbor Springs, Petoskey, and Bay Harbor are scenic towns definitely worth visiting by water or land.

In 1998, Elaine and I set Lake Michigan and Green Bay as our summer goal to explore in our 370 Sea Ray Express Cruiser. We would combine it with a family gathering in a cottage Elaine rented on Lake Charlevoix for a week in July.

Our son Craig and daughter-in-law Susan flew from California to Pellston Regional Airport, south of the Mackinac Bridge, and we met them in St. Ignace. After spending a day on Mackinac Island, we departed for Lake Charlevoix and the cottage, which we reached in less than three hours.

After a leisurely cruise, we entered Round Lake, located in downtown Charlevoix, then passed through it into the south arm of Lake Charlevoix. Since we had only a street address, we were challenged to find the cottage from the water approach, but perseverance prevailed, and we tied off at the cottage's dock. The rest of the family arrived from Ohio, the Upper Peninsula of Michigan, and lower Michigan for the week-long family get-together.

We hated to have our time together end, but after a fantastic week with all the family, Elaine and I took my sister Trish on board the ELEANA for our departure, with Beaver Island as our first destination. The 370 ran at twenty-two miles an hour, so we entered the St. James Harbor after thirty-two miles, in less than two hours. That July day was ideal, with warm sunshine and seas of only one to two feet.

Beaver Island is Lake Michigan's largest island. Although nowadays it is a vacation resort with only six hundred year-round residents, it accommodates many more in the Michigan summers. St. James is the island's only town. But Beaver Island has an extraordinary history.

Indigenous people inhabited Beaver Island perhaps as far back as 11,000 years ago, fishing and fur-trapping. The earliest traces of their culture were found in the 1980s, along Angeline's Bluff, where an archeologist discovered a long-forgotten circle of thirty-nine glacial boulders centered on a boulder with a hole carved in it. The boulders range in height from two to ten feet and form a nearly perfect 397-foot circle, with unusual carvings on the surface. Research is still ongoing to determine the origins of the circle, but most believe it was created 4,500 years ago for a Native American ceremonial use. A smaller circle was subsequently found elsewhere on the island. The

# "Lake Michigan is now called the Deadliest Great Lake, because more people have drowned in its waters than in any of the other Great Lakes."

oldest artifacts archeologists have discovered date from 1,200 years ago, but the natives who used them vanished before the Ojibwa arrived.

After the War of 1812, the island's rich fishing grounds attracted Irish settlers, who fished from small sailboats and traded with the Ojibwa. Then, in 1847, James Jesse Strang moved onto the island with the Strangites, a group of Mormons who had split from the Latter Day Saints after Joseph Smith's death. Strang became America's first and only king, having himself crowned "King of Land and Sea" on the island. The Mormon community grew to 2,000, despite hostility with the Irish settlers and fishermen. In 1856, Strang was murdered. Within weeks, his followers were driven away, and the Irish fishermen reclaimed Beaver Island.

When we left St. James, we entered scenic Green Bay and continued up the bay to Escanaba, where my sister met her friend and headed home to Marquette. The next morning, Elaine and I cruised south along the coast to Marinette, Wisconsin, where I wanted to observe the Bay Shipbuilding Companies' operations, both in Marinette and Sturgeon Bay.

The Marinette operation sits on the Menominee River, which is the border between Michigan's Upper Peninsula and Wisconsin. The Sturgeon Bay operation is on the Door Peninsula separating Green Bay and Lake Michigan. With a history dating back to 1918, the Bay Shipbuilding Company is owned and operated by the Fincantieri Marine Group, a world leader in shipbuilding and repair. The Marinette operation recently received contracts to design and build ten frigates for the U.S. Navy, with the first delivery scheduled for 2026. A frigate is five hundred feet long and sixty feet wide, so these ships will be able to pass through the Welland Canal on their way to the Atlantic Ocean.

The Sturgeon Bay site also builds the one-thousand-foot-long lake freighters that are used exclusively on the Great Lakes, as well as other huge carriers and equipment. This operation is located on the Door County Peninsula in the southern part of the Green Bay. A canal connects Sturgeon Bay with Lake Michigan and provides a waterway across the Door County peninsula between Lake Michigan and Green Bay.

Our next goal was to visit the west coast of the Door County Peninsula, which some call "the Cape Cod of the Midwest." Its history is rich with Ojibwa lore, French explorers, Jesuit missionaries, sailors, and fur traders.

The French named the dangerous passage, or strait, between the peninsula and Washington Island Porte des Morts (Death's Door), which is how Door County got its name. Numerous shipwrecks attest to its maritime challenges.

Early settlers lumbered and fished, and our thoughts were on fish when we made our first stop at Fish Creek Marina. Fish Creek is located along Green Bay, a picturesque village with galleries, boat tours, beaches, lighthouses, fine dining, and art galleries.

*Our boating adventures began with a 32-foot Sea Ray. In time, we moved up to this $1.5 million 57 Bertram, the largest boat we ever captained.*

Next, we moved to Sister Bay. Renting a car, we drove throughout the scenic peninsula and enjoyed one of Door County's famous fish boils.

On our way back to Lake Erie, we cruised through Gray's Reef, a charted deeper water area on the lake between Beaver Island and the northwest shore of Michigan's Lower Peninsula. We continued on to the Straits of Mackinac and cruised under the five-mile Mackinac Bridge to St. Ignace. After an overnight in St. Ignace, we couldn't resist spending several nights on Mackinac Island before heading back home.

Lake Michigan has the third-largest surface area of the Great Lakes, but is second in depth, at 925 feet. Lying in a north-south position, the lake is 307 miles long, 118 miles wide at its widest point, and ninety-one miles wide at the narrowest. Boaters know about its three segments, each having different characteristics. Green Bay is north and west of the main body of water. Grand Traverse Bay is situated on the north and east end of the main body of the lake. And Beaver, North Manitou, and South Manitou islands are located off Michigan's northwest shore, along with six smaller islands.

Lake Michigan's waters are channeled through the five-mile-wide Straits of Mackinac into Lake Huron. Ecologists estimate that Lake Michigan's water is replaced every one hundred years—and since it borders large urban centers and industrial areas, it has struggled with pollution and refuse for two centuries, primarily due to Chicago's drainage and Gary, Indiana's steel mills.

Those pollutants move three hundred miles north before finally exiting from Lake Michigan. I have concluded that the pollutants and sewage from Chicago emitted in the year 1900 finally left Lake Michigan in the year 2000, moving into Lake Huron. In 2025, they were about to enter Lake Erie.

The Ice Age created a five-mile-wide watershed area whose line stretches from what is now Waukegan to South Chicago, Illinois.

This narrow watershed created the Chicago River and its tributaries, all of which flow into Lake Michigan. The line passes through downtown Chicago. The water from rain and snow on the west side of the shed line flows westward on the Des Plaines River, into the Illinois River, and finally down the Mississippi River. All the surface water on the east side of the watershed line flows into Lake Michigan.

As Chicago and the adjoining areas expanded during the 19th century, all of the pollutants and sewage (including carcasses from its meat-packing plants) from the east side of the watershed flowed into the Chicago River and its tributaries, and then directly into Lake Michigan. The human and cattle stockyard contaminants were disastrous to the entire southern end of Lake Michigan—not to mention to the area's residents.

In the year 1900, Chicago dug a canal through the natural watershed high ground, diverting the Chicago River and its tributaries into the Des Plaines River and on to the Mississippi River. This Chicago Sanitary Canal has a single lock preventing the contaminated water from entering Lake Michigan and providing access to the Mississippi River from Lake Michigan, thereby reducing the lake's contamination. Pleasure craft from the Great Lakes can now pass through Illinois into the Mississippi River, travel down to the Gulf of Mexico, over to the Atlantic, up the East Coast, and return back into the Great Lakes by way of the Hudson River and Erie Barge Canal. This passage is called The Great Loop—a challenge many experienced boaters have dreamed of, including yours truly.

Michigan's western shoreline has traditionally attracted the Midwest's wealthy residents to its scenic resort towns. Farther north, the lands bordering the state's western shore are renowned for their fruit crops. Cherries, apples, peaches, grapes (and, consequently, wine-making) thrive in this climate. The lake effect sends hundreds of inches of snow each winter, which is appreciated by winter sports enthusiasts.

Lake Michigan is now called the Deadliest Great Lake, because more people have drowned in its waters than in any of the other Great Lakes. The waves of Lake Michigan quickly build to great heights because of the lake's long north-to-south position on the earth combined with the predominately westerly winds. As the population of western Michigan has boomed, many newcomers and new boaters are unaware of the notorious sudden weather changes, which create those huge waves with deadly rip currents.

In my career as a delivery captain, Marine Max's operations in Wisconsin and Minnesota handled the majority of the boat business for Lake Michigan. However, Elaine and I delivered boats to Hammond, Indiana; Sheboygan, Wisconsin; and Michigan City, Michigan over the years. Those deliveries, plus our personal cruising experiences, provided most of our experiences on Lake Michigan. ■

> "Pleasure craft from the Great Lakes can now pass through Illinois into the Mississippi River, travel down to the Gulf of Mexico, over to the Atlantic, up the East Coast, and return back into the Great Lakes by way of the Hudson River and Erie Barge Canal."

*Captain Pat sits at the helm of our 400 Sea Ray during a voyage across smooth waters.*

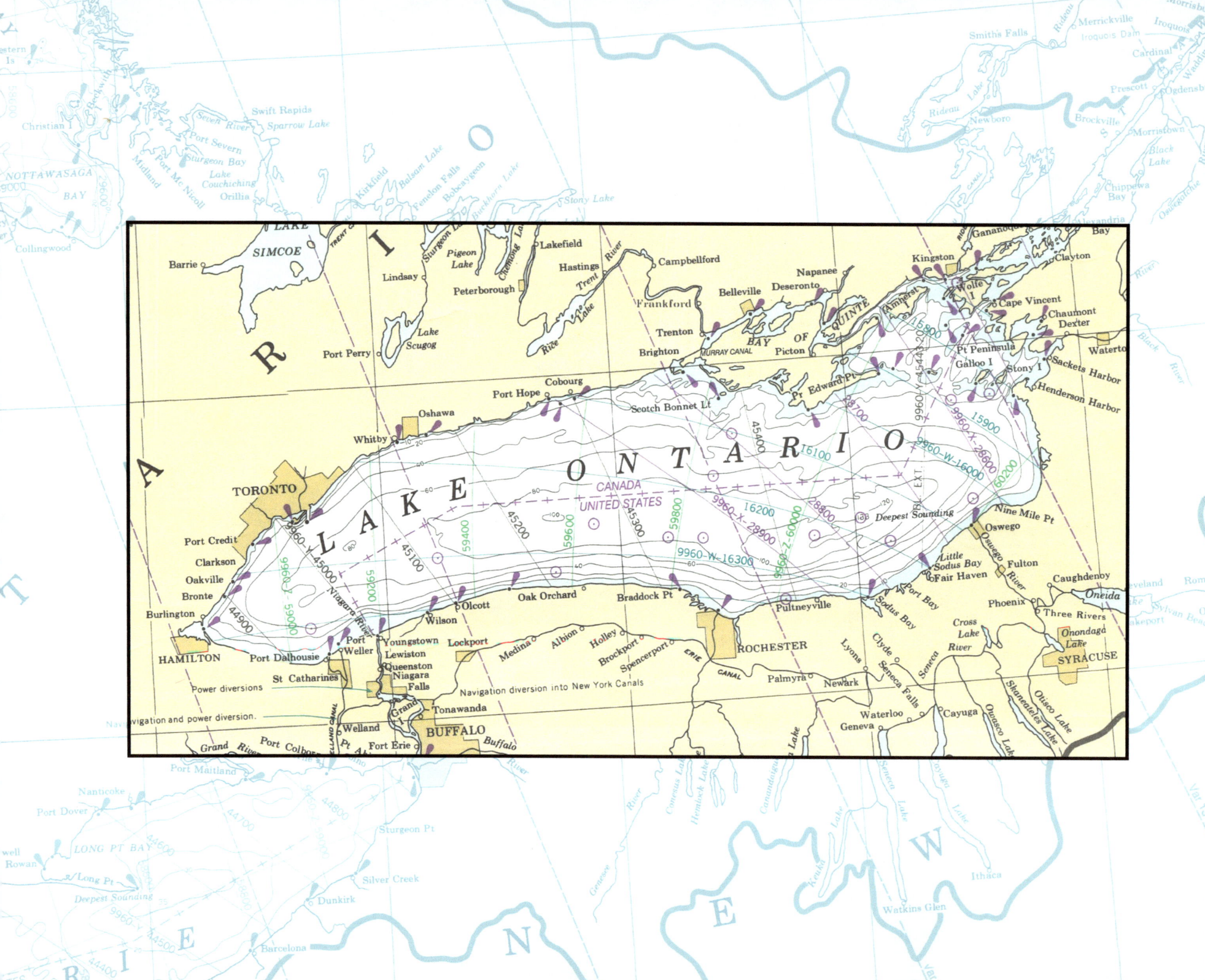

## CHAPTER 8
# Exploring the Welland Canal, Lake Ontario, and St. Lawrence River

**IN THE SUMMER** of 1996, only four years after buying our first Great Lakes boat, we moved up to a 1964 370 Sea Ray Express Cruiser, which convinced us that we might be ready to explore the fifth—and our last—Great Lake: Lake Ontario.

We studied the charts and discovered we would have to pass through Canada's twenty-three-mile Welland Canal on our way. Our boat would have to be lowered 326 feet in seven forty-six-foot steps down to Lake Ontario. We would, of course, have to be lifted back into Lake Erie on our return journey. This new unknown was both very scary and challenging for us.

Would it take days or only hours to complete? What preparations would we have to make? Would we be sharing a lock with a lake or ocean freighter? All unanswered questions. So far.

Up to this time, our only lock experience was the single twenty-five-foot lock entering and leaving Lake Superior, which was a basic and simple process. But I was determined to expand our knowledge and experience on all the Great Lakes.

We quizzed boating friends, asking if they had passed through the canal, but we couldn't find anyone who had done it. Tom, the manager of Treasure Cove Marina, heard we were making these plans and volunteered his experience. He had passed through the Welland Canal as a passenger on a pleasure craft bound for Florida. He didn't recall a lot of detail, but said he didn't think we would have any problems. However, he hadn't experienced the return trip, where the boat would be raised 326 feet in the seven locks. Nor had he waited in the turbulent waters of forty-seven-foot-deep locks as the giant bathtubs were being filled with water in order raise the boats.

Not very much information, but we were determined to go. We started to plan by reading as much information as we could find.

The 189-mile St. Lawrence River Seaway connects the Atlantic Ocean through the St. Lawrence Bay and River to Lake Ontario. This is the only commercial waterway connection between the Atlantic and the Great Lakes. The Seaway begins in Montreal and proceeds through five Canadian and two American locks that lift and lower vessels 246 feet, the difference between the Atlantic Ocean and Lake Ontario. More than two hundred million tons of cargo move through this watery transportation system per year.

The Niagara River is the ancient link between Lake Erie and Lake Ontario. It passes through rapids to finally cascade over the 160-foot Niagara Falls.

The Canadians constructed a canal in 1829, to bypass Niagara Falls and lift and lower vessels between Lake Ontario and Lake Erie, but it was abandoned when the Welland Canal was completed in 1932. Engineers deepened the system in the 1950s, and straightened it in 1973.

The Welland consists of seven locks, each averaging forty-six feet of water necessary for lifting or lowering vessels. The locks are numbered, beginning at Lake Ontario. An eighth lock is only used

*After four years of boating on the Great Lakes, we purchased a 1964 370 Sea Ray Express Cruiser and decided we were ready to explore our fifth Great Lake: Ontario.*

when the water level in Lake Erie is higher than normal. In our twelve years and thirteen trips passing through the Welland, we only used Lock 8 twice.

Each lock is 766 feet long and eighty feet wide. The depth throughout the canal is thirty feet.

## OUR FIRST PASSAGE

Our first overnight on our eastward cruise was a repeat visit to the Old River Yacht Club in Cleveland, located in the back waters of the Cleveland Harbor. Based on our prior experience, we knew it provides a safe and secure location with locked gates to reduce public traffic. The club dining room was well decorated, and the kitchen provided excellent dinners.

Our next planned overnight was our first visit to Erie, Pennsylvania, and we wanted to check out the harbor for possible future visits.

The city of Erie is located on the lake's Presque Isle Bay, which is about four miles long and two miles wide. The bay is protected by the Presque Isle land extending from the west mainland shore to the only entrance on the east end of the bay.

After entering the bay, we slowly moved down the row of available marinas and dockage. Looking farther west, I noticed the Erie Yacht Club on the far west end of the bay. Elaine called the marina and asked if they accepted transient docking. The immediate response: "We certainly do. We have fuel, and someone will be there to provide the fuel and direct you to a dock." We were also invited to enjoy the dining room.

After fueling and moving to our designated dock, we met our dockmate couple. Sharing glasses of wine, we didn't take very long before asking about the Welland Canal. The immediate response was, "Yes, we have passed through it at least a dozen times."

We had included extra fenders in our onboard inventory, but our new friends suggested, "Old-time gunny sacks filled with straw will work so much better. They absorb the energy when the boat is suddenly thrown back against the lock wall by the turbulent water leaving or entering the lock." They added that men sell those gunny sacks at each end of the canal, and we could find experienced boaters there to hire, to accompany us along the canal.

"You must have three people on board to man the boat when going through the Welland. One person on the bow, one at the stern, and the captain at the helm."

They recommended we stay overnight at Marlon Marina in Port Colborne, which is adjacent to the entrance into the Welland Canal from Lake Erie. "The crossing will most likely take a full day," they advised us. "After clearing Lock 1, you'll be in Port Weller, but there are no accommodations there, so enter Lake Ontario and go north a short distance to the Port Dalhousie Marina to stay overnight."

We were very grateful for their detailed advice. The couple asked us to join them for dinner at the Erie Yacht Club, and we enjoyed a wonderful evening there. We thanked them for all the information, and as we retired, we thanked the Lord for sending this couple to calm our anxious thoughts.

Upon arriving at Marlon Marina in Port Colborne, we docked and used the special phone in the Marlon Marina building to register with Canadian Customs and Immigration. This was a well-known process, as we often visited Leamington, on the north shore of Lake Erie.

After registering for a dock, we met the manager of the marina and asked if he knew of an experienced person to accompany us through the canal. We also inquired about the straw bags.

"A number of men provide this service, but since you're new to the canal, I recommend Dan, a young man attending a local college. He has extensive experience with the canal, and this job helps him with his college expenses."

I called Dan, and he said he was available for tomorrow's pass through the canal. He also had straw bags, which he immediately brought to the marina. He not only demonstrated where they would be installed, but assisted us in installing them on ELEANA. Elaine and I were very impressed with Dan. He reminded us of our sons.

When we asked about compensation, Dan explained that the time for the trip through the canal was extremely unpredictable,

*With excitement and some trepidation, I prepared to enter the Welland Canal for our first time.*

and he described some of his experiences. He said he normally set a rate based on a twelve-hour pass through, sometimes less and sometimes more. We agreed if the time was more than normal, we would compensate beyond the standard rate.

We agreed to meet in the canal queuing area at seven o'clock the next morning. Dan also explained that before his arrival we should pay for our passage, and he would assist us when with the registration through the canal.

"Then we'll wait for the call to proceed. If there are other pleasure craft going with us, the canal scheduler will group us and assign each boat to a specific position for traversing together."

Before departing, Dan outlined the process of being lowered the 326 feet from Lake Erie to Lake Ontario, and what to expect during the removal of water from the lock.

Elaine and I went through a fitful night. We didn't sleep well, as we anticipated what could happen in this totally new adventure.

> "We finalized our plans for our first cruise in Canada and the areas we hoped to explore along the north shore of Lake Ontario and the St. Lawrence River."

The next morning, we were at the queuing dock before seven o'clock and paid the required fees through the automated system. When Dan arrived at seven sharp, I called to notify Welland we were ready. And then we waited. Finally, the VHF announced we would begin at 9:45. With bated breath and some fears, we were underway.

As we moved from the dock into the channel, Welland Control announced, "ELEANA, you are assigned to the lead position with five sailboats. Never shut off the engines, since a maneuver might suddenly be required. Wait for the lock doors to be fully open before exiting."

We passed right through the open Lock 8 without any change in water elevation. Continuing at no-wake, we slowly moved eighteen miles to Lock 7, with the sailboats trailing behind. Since we were going down the 326 feet into Lake Ontario, each of the locks would be filled to the brim as we entered. We were told to proceed forward to the far end of the south wall, where two men stood with coiled lines, which they handed to Elaine at the bow and Dan at the stern.

While we waited for the five sailboats to enter and receive their lines, Dan demonstrated how the lines were to be cleated so they would slip through the cleat as we dropped with the water level. He then showed how to tie off with one quick move to lock the line to the boat, should it be required to secure the boat to the south wall.

After all the boats were in the lock and the lock doors were closed, we started to lower as the water was released. It took twenty-five minutes on average for the water to be completely expelled and the boats lowered forty-six feet. We then waited for the lock doors to fully open before leaving.

Departing from Lock 7, we proceeded one mile in the channel to Lock 6. Repeating the process, we proceeded a half-mile to Lock 5, a half-mile to Lock 4, one mile to Lock 3, a half-mile to Lock 2, and, finally, two miles to Lock 1.

When we left Lock 1, we were in Port Weller, Ontario. It was 5:30 at night, so our travel time was seven hours and thirty minutes after waiting three hours before starting our first Welland adventure. Astonishing to think we had been lowered 326 feet!

Maneuvering ELEANA out of the sailboats' way, we stopped briefly to celebrate our first successful traverse through the Welland before entering into our fifth Great Lake. The three of us shared hugs and high-fives.

The entrance to the Welland, Port Weller is at the same level as Lake Ontario. At a docking area on the south wall, boaters register with Canadian Customs and Immigration if entering Canada from New York State. The same site collects the fee for traversing the Welland. Once these preparations are completed, all boaters must wait for the call to begin the ascent to Lake Erie.

Dan stayed on board as we exited Port Weller, turned north, and headed to Port Dalhousie Marina. He assisted us with docking at Port Dalhousie Marina and said he would assist us on our return up the Welland.

We finalized our plans for our first stay in Canada and the areas we hoped to explore along the north shore of Lake Ontario and the St. Lawrence River. We would then enter the U.S.A. and explore the south shore of the St. Lawrence River. After circumnavigating Lake Ontario, we would reenter Canada at Port Weller for the ascent to

*After stopping in Toronto, we decided the marina was too busy and headed to the Toronto islands.*

Lake Erie. This trip would prepare us for future travels and expand our knowledge and capabilities.

We stayed for two nights in Port Dalhousie, enjoying the chance to visit and explore the area and its restaurants. To reach the town, we had to use our inflatable dingy to paddle across the river that separated the marina from the downtown area. We admired the landscape along the way. The Canadians certainly know how to grow and display flowers. Elaine especially enjoyed their numerous varieties and beauty. More flower varieties for her garden and more work for me.

Our next stop was Toronto and its downtown marina, but after entering, we decided it was too busy. While we waited for fuel, a local boater suggested we stay on Lake Ontario's Toronto Islands, located about a mile directly south of the City Marina.

What a beautiful place! We had loaded our folding bikes on board the boat, and we rode all over the island. My overall impression was an island covered with flowers. Elaine's love of gardening made our two-day stay very enjoyable. We also rode the island's ferry to visit downtown Toronto, where we shopped and ate a delicious lunch on the waterfront.

The next stop on the north shore was Cobourg. Again, so many flowers and a spectacular sunset.

To enter the United States, we crossed the entrance of the St. Lawrence River to Cape Vincent, New York, at the start of the St. Lawrence River on its way to the Atlantic Ocean. This area is known as the Thousand Islands.

Here we learned about the famous Boldt Castle on an island in the St. Lawrence across from Alexander Bay. Elaine said she wanted to visit the castle, so we started down the St. Lawerence River until we found a dock in Alexander Bay. We spent several fun-filled days exploring the area.

Millionaire George C. Boldt started building Boldt Castle in 1900, as a gift for his wife. Three hundred workers labored on the six-story, 120-room castle for four years. Tragically, before it was completed, Louise Boldt died. George suspended all work on the castle and never again returned to the property.

*Flower gardens were in full bloom wherever we went that summer.*

Nowadays, Boldt is remembered for two things: he was responsible for joining the Waldorf and Astoria hotels into the renowned Waldorf-Astoria Hotel in New York City, and he is credited with inventing the Thousand Island salad dressing.

Our remaining agenda on Lake Ontario was to circumnavigate the lake. This included stopping in Oswego, New York, where the Oswego River enters Lake Ontario. The river's seven locks carry pleasure craft 118 feet up to the Erie Barge Canal.

While docked at the Oswego Marina, we walked into the city to view Lock 8. (There are only seven active locks on the Oswego River; number 4 no longer exists.) We learned what we would encounter if we chose to travel the Oswego River as far as the Erie Barge Canal, should we ever decide to continue down to the Hudson River and out to the Atlantic Ocean.

We decided we would spend our last night in Youngstown, New York, as it would be only a few miles away from the Welland entrance. Youngstown is where the Niagara River enters Lake Ontario, serving as the border between United States and Canada.

When we entered the river, we discovered a beautiful marina on the Canadian side, in the village of Niagara-on-the-Lake, where we docked. We would be ready to enter the canal at Port Weller in the morning.

We phoned Dan and arranged to have him meet us at seven in the morning at Port Weller, bringing bags of straw with him.

*Elaine and I packed foldable bikes on board, so we could enjoy exploring harbors, gardens, and attractions on our cruise among the Thousand Islands.*

The next morning, Dan arrived as scheduled, and I checked in with Welland Control, but we didn't receive a go-ahead into Lock 1 until 11:20. Welland Control notified us that we were the only vessel transversing, and we should expect to be tying off in the center of each of the locks.

Entering the empty Lock 1, I was amazed at the size of this forty-six-foot walled bath tub. When the doors closed, it felt like we were on a tiny boat. The high-pressure pumps suddenly turned on, and the water entered with extreme turbulence, boiling and splashing. Our boat was literally thrown around in the lock, and I had to use the propellers to reduce our movement. The fore and aft lines handled by Elaine and Dan had to be held tight to keep ELEANA close to the south wall, even though Welland Control had placed us in the center of the lock's south wall, the area with the least turbulence.

This process was repeated six more times before finally exiting the twenty-three-mile Welland Canal at five o'clock. A ten-hour experience to return to Lake Erie.

The next day at Port Colborne, we found that our air conditioning unit was not working and the circuit breaker kept opening whenever I reset it. I hired a technician to check out the unit, but he couldn't find the problem, so I spent the rest of day taking apart the water intake system used for pumping water through our air conditioning and heating units. This way, I discovered a piece of straw jammed between the pump impeller and the pump housing.

After I removed the straw and reassembled the unit, our air conditioning performed perfectly. The next time we went through the Welland, we were told that straw bags were forbidden in the canal. I believe we weren't the only boaters or canal operation to find straw shutting down water pumps.

We were proud to have cruised through the Welland Canal and down the St. Lawrence River, as well as circumnavigating Lake Ontario. Many of our boating friends were envious of our accomplishment. I added this success to my list of experiences pursuing excellence in boating. ■

*The 120-room Boldt Castle was nearly complete in 1904, when millionaire George C. Boldt lost his wife, Louise, and he immediately ended all work on the castle and never returned again.*

DEPT. OF HOMELAND SECURITY, U.S. COAST GUARD, CG-2849 (REV. 6-04)

SERIAL NUMBER
1197883

ISSUE NUMBER 3

# UNITED STATES COAST GUARD LICENSE

# U.S. MERCHANT MARINE OFFICER

*This is to certify that*

**\*\*\* WILBUR PATRICK WINTON \*\*\***

*having been duly examined and found competent by the undersigned is licensed to serve for the term of five years from the below issue date as:*

MASTER OF STEAM OR MOTOR VESSELS OF NOT MORE THAN 100 GROSS REGISTERED TONS (DOMESTIC TONNAGE) UPON GREAT LAKES AND INLAND WATERS; ALSO, AUTHORIZED TO ENGAGE IN COMMERCIAL ASSISTANCE TOWING.

*Given under my hand this* 13th *day of* January 2008.

*E. M. Bibee*

ISSUE PORT: TOLEDO, OH
EXPIRATION DATE: JANUARY 13, 2013

E. M. BIBEE, USCG, BY DIRECTION
OFFICER IN CHARGE, MARINE INSPECTION

## CHAPTER 9
# Our New Careers: Delivery Captain & First Mate

**RETIREMENT MEANS** something different for everyone. For Elaine and for me, it meant more time to explore America's waterways.

In 1999, we agreed I would retire from my forty-two-year career in engineering management in 2004, giving us five years to plan and prepare for our retirement. The initial step was to choose and purchase our retirement boat and then find property and build a home on Catawba Island in Port Clinton, Ohio.

With these decisions made, we needed a larger boat that would fit our second-career dreams, provide more amenities on board, and extend our range and weather capability on the water. We were dreaming of spending a winter on our boat while completing the six-thousand-mile Great Loop, taking us from the Great Lakes down the Mississippi, into the Gulf of Mexico, around Florida, and back up the Atlantic.

After researching various boats, we decided to find and purchase a used Sea Ray 400 with twin diesels. Our search began.

In October of 1999, we were heading to Chicago for a board meeting when Elaine read the mail we had grabbed from our mailbox just before we left home. As we approached the Indiana border on the turnpike, she announced, "Here's a used one-year-old 1998 Sea Ray 400 with twin diesels and low hours. It's located in Michigan City, on Lake Michigan! Didn't we just pass the exit for Michigan City?"

Immediately, she called the marina and asked about the boat. We made an appointment to view it on our return trip from Chicago three days later.

That Sea Ray was exactly what we wanted. We agreed on a deal on our way home. It involved a lot of details, since we were trading in

> "In January of 2001, in preparation for my official retirement at age sixty-five in 2004, I initiated my dream to obtain a U.S. Coast Guard license."

> "Our goal was for me to become the best and most experienced captain on the Great Lakes and for Elaine to become the best and most experienced first mate on the Great Lakes and inland waters."

our 370 Sea Ray and would have to arrange land transportation for both boats, the 400 from Michigan City to Ohio, and the 370 from Ohio to Michigan City.

As soon as our new boat arrived on Catawba Island, we placed it in heated winter storage and spent the winter preparing for its spring launch in 2000.

In January of 2001, in preparation for my official retirement at age sixty-five in 2004, I initiated my dream to obtain a U.S. Coast Guard license. I enrolled in the United States Coast Guard License training program.

At that time, the Coast Guard offered two license options, first to become an Operator of Uninspected Passenger Vessels (O.U.P.V.), often referred to as SIXPAC because it allowed six paying customers, and the second was a Master of Inspected Vessels license, with an unlimited number of paying customers on vessels up to one hundred tons. The second was my goal.

I found an approved Captain's School in the Cleveland, Ohio area offering the approved courses and examinations. I attended three consecutive weekends of classes on Fridays, Saturdays, and Sundays, and successfully passed the tests for a SIXPAC license.

The fourth weekend, I attended the Master's Upgrade three-day weekend course and successfully passed those tests. A few weeks later, I received my official certification: MASTER OF STEAM OR MOTOR VESSELS OF NOT MORE THAN 100 GROSS TONS (DOMESTIC TONNAGE) UPON THE GREAT LAKES AND INLAND WATERS, ALSO AUTHORIZATION TO ENGAGE IN COMMERCIAL ASSISTANCE TOWING.

To complete our retirement plan, we purchased a lot on Catawba Island that year. Our retirement home was completed in 2003.

In the eleven years between 1992 and 2003, we continued to expand our on-the-water capability and experience. Our goal was for me to become the best and most experienced captain on the Great Lakes and for Elaine to become the best and most experienced first mate on the Great Lakes and inland waters.

Now new opportunities, challenges, and greater responsibilities opened to us as my retirement date approached. ∎

*I fulfilled a life-long goal when the U.S. Coast Guard awarded me a master's license for inspected vessels, and I officially became Captain Pat. This launched my second career, this one on the water.*

Elaine and I had meticulously researched possible waterways for our Great Loop adventure, planning which lock systems, marinas, and towns we would use on the journey. But we learned that the best-laid plans don't always come to fruition.

## CHAPTER 10
# Our Disastrous Great Loop Voyage

IN ONLY THE THIRD hour of our 2004 Great Loop Winter Cruise, we were cruising on the straight stretch of the Detroit River between Fighting Island and Wyandotte when the boat was suddenly shaken by a loud BANG! The explosion seemed to originate in the engine compartment, and the starboard engine immediately went to maximum rpm.

I instantly shut down the engine and rushed into the engine compartment, fearing fire. But, thank the Lord, I discovered no fire and no water intrusion.

When I raced back to the helm, Elaine yelled, "What happened?"

"I don't know, but NO fire or water in the engine compartment! We need to find a place to tie off and check everything. We only have the port engine for power."

Because we were in the four-mile-per-hour river current, we slowly maneuvered upstream using only the port engine. Turning into the Wyandotte Channel, Elaine pointed to a marine fuel dock. After entering and tying off, I started the starboard engine and tried to shift the transmission, but received no response. Did we hit something? Lose the propeller? What's wrong?

The fuel attendant came and asked if we needed fuel. When I explained what happened in the Detroit River, he told us there was a boat repair operation a short distance down the channel. "Stay here. I'll run and get their number," he said as he ran to the fuel dock office.

When I called, they told me to bring ELEANA over and go directly into the lift well. Elaine looked at me with tears, pointing out, "And we're only getting started."

In the summer of 2004, after completing my engineering management career and retiring that June, I embarked upon a new career as a licensed U. S. Coast Guard Captain with a 100-ton rating. Living on the Great Lakes, we had been considering what we might do with our free time in the winter of 2004-05, and Elaine and I discussed whether we should undertake a major challenge.

"Elaine, should we consider taking our ELEANA on the six-thousand-mile Great Loop Journey?" I suggested one day. Before she could answer, I hurried to continue, "If so, we would have to leave the Great Lakes in September and enter the Chicago Sanitary Canal from Lake Michigan. We'd reach the Mississippi River via the Des Plains and Illinois Rivers, end in New Orleans, and then cruise over to the Florida Keys, where we could spend the winter months."

Elaine finally found her voice. "Pat, you can't be serious! We would be gone for eight months!"

"Let's plan to do it. What an adventure!" I urged.

Elaine was obviously very hesitant and brought up numerous what "ifs" and "maybes," but finally agreed.

Maybe I should have listened to her!

*Off we go! On August 23, 2004, we started off on our Great Loop adventure, with detailed plans and high hopes. This was the first year of my retirement.*

That's how the plan began. We started from the beginning of the journey and talked our way through the numerous steps, after spending hours reviewing happy and horror stories, selecting which rivers or canals to use, and outlining a timeline based on weather and accommodations.

We found we would have to leave the Great Lakes before the end of September, as most of the marinas on the Great Lakes and the Illinois River shut down after Labor Day, and we certainly wouldn't want to encounter any of the infamous Great Lakes fall storms.

Our trip would begin by going around Michigan, down to Chicago, and into the Chicago Sanitary and Ship Canal, which connects with the Des Plains River. The Des Plains River empties into the Illinois River, and after passing through eight locks, we would enter the Mississippi River.

I didn't want to be in the Gulf of Mexico until well into December, so we would avoid the gulf's potential November/December hurricane season. Taking the dirty Mississippi River to New Orleans would be difficult with all the large ships and barge traffic going up and down

> "So, we spent the summer of 2004 doing massive research on potential marinas, studying what types of bad weather we might encounter, what clothes we would need, and the special charts and navigation information the Great Loop would require."

the river. Also, according to the experienced boaters, marinas are more difficult to find along the way.

We decided we would be safer and find more available marinas in Tennessee or Alabama in October and November. We would have to leave the Mississippi where the Ohio River enters it and travel up the Ohio to Paduca, Kentucky. There we could enter the Tennessee-Tombigbee Waterway, which would be cleaner water and safer passage, with numerous marinas in Tennessee and Alabama.

The Tennessee-Tombigbee Waterway runs parallel to the Mississippi River, and we decided that would be an enjoyable area of the country to spend October and November. When ready to move south, we could continue down the Tombigbee River through Mobile, Alabama, and into the Gulf of Mexico.

Our close friends on Catawba Island spent their winters in Key Colony Beach on Marathon Key, one of the Florida Keys. They were acquainted with the manager of a marina there, who said we could rent a dock for the first couple months of the new year.

Other close friends, an Ohio couple, had purchased a home on the intercoastal just north of Miami. They offered the use of their dock, so we could tie off for a month or so before heading homeward.

Returning north along the East Coast of the Atlantic Ocean, we would need to arrive in New York Harbor for the opening of the Erie Barge Canal, which normally occurred in mid-May. The canal begins at the Hudson River in Troy, New York and ends in Buffalo. We wouldn't be able to reach Buffalo, though. Instead, we planned to take the Oswego River down to Lake Ontario. Height clearances between Oswego River and Buffalo would restrict ELEANA from passing through this segment of the Erie Barge Canal.

I assured Elaine we would be home by the end of May, just in time to head north on the Great Lakes.

Our Great Loop plan was beginning to develop and make sense. And, whenever we started to get cold feet, I would repeat, "We always have the option to put ELEANA on a trailer and have her hauled home."

So, we spent the summer of 2004 doing massive research on potential marinas, studying what types of bad weather we might encounter, what clothes would we need, and the special charts and navigation information the Great Loop would require. I purchased special tools and spare parts, everything from water-cooling pump impellers to belts, filters, and special batteries. I had a special air horn installed so we would be certain to be heard in case of an emergency. Our dinghy and outboard were thoroughly checked.

We then tackled the practical aspects of nine months away from home. Arrangements were defined and assigned for mail to be collected and forwarded, a means of communication with our scattered family members established, and arrangements finalized for the care of our property and payment procedures for home services and taxes.

We were ready!

## WE ARE ON OUR WAY

Knowing we had to exit Lake Michigan by mid-September, we left our yacht club on Lake Erie at ten o'clock on the morning of August 23, 2004, with a great sense of adventure and excitement. Our plan called for us to spend a month on the Great Lakes, to see the fall colors before entering the rivers.

During the first half hour of our first day, we were cruising on calm seas at twenty-seven miles per hour when I suddenly smelled diesel fuel. Panicking, imagining fire or fuel oil on the water, I immediately cut the engines and headed to the engine compartment, where I saw diesel fuel sloshing in the bilge.

Elaine hurriedly opened the locker to grab the bags of fuel diapers we always kept for such an emergency. I dropped down into the engine compartment and grabbed the buckets I kept there for emergencies. My immediate impulse was to get the fuel into the buckets before the bilge pumps began spewing the diesel into the lake, creating a fuel-spill catastrophe.

Frantically I searched for a reason for the problem. I found the generator fuel filter leaking where the filter threads into the fuel pump. The threads were stripped, and I had no way to tighten the filter. Anxiously reaching for the shut-off valve, I discovered I couldn't reach it, thanks to a faulty design, so I turned my attention to the fuel sloshing in the bilge.

Elaine called Treasure Cove, screaming for immediate assistance while I scooped and absorbed as much diesel as I could get into my five-gallon bucket. Hurrying back to the helm, I started the engines and raced back to CIC Yacht Club, where two Marine Max technicians were waiting at the fuel dock. They immediately jumped on board and shut off the fuel to the generator. To my great relief, I realized no diesel fuel had been pumped overboard!

We couldn't find spare parts for the generator fuel filter assembly anywhere on the southwest shore of Lake Erie. Eventually we were informed that the nearest spare parts were available at the generator factory on the St. Clair River in Marysville, Michigan. We made a reservation for that night at the St. Clair City Marina, and I made arrangements for the repairs to be done there the following day.

The Treasure Cove service manager arrived, made certain everything was cleaned up, and apologized profusely for the stripped threads and the failure to check their installation. He showed me the necessary maneuvers to reach the fuel shut-off to the generator.

I was ashamed that I hadn't mastered this very basic safety maneuver on my own boat. In my future career of boarding and moving boats, finding and manually reaching the shut-off valves was one of the first basic checks I made before starting engines.

At noon, we once again set out on our Great Loop cruise. The seas were only one to two feet, and we soon entered the Detroit River, cruising at about twenty-eight miles per hour. The afternoon was still beautiful and sunny when the sudden explosion in the engine compartment occurred.

## BACK TO THE THIRD HOUR OF OUR GREAT LOOP CRUISE

The Wyandotte boat repair technician lifted ELEANA out of the water, but couldn't find anything wrong with the starboard propeller or shaft. He moved aboard and checked out the transmission, then concluded the internal gears had failed. "We can't help you—we don't work on this type of pleasure craft," he informed us. "You're welcome to stay overnight in the boat well, since we don't have anyone coming in the morning, so no need to rush."

I only knew of one place to obtain repairs of this magnitude: Colony Marine, the Sea Ray dealership in St. Clair Shores on Lake

*Our gearbox was the source of Disaster #2 of Day #1. Only one replacement starboard gearbox existed, and it was in Ft. Lauderdale.*

St. Clair. I called and arranged to arrive the following afternoon. We would be traveling twenty-five miles on one engine.

The night was terrible, with little sleep, as we wondered why so many problems had befallen us on the first day of our Great Loop cruise. In our twelve years of boating on the Great Lakes, we had never experienced two major problems in a single day.

Little did we know that was only the beginning.

The following morning, we set out to Lake St. Clair right after breakfast. We moved very slowly, since the single port engine was pushing the twelve-ton ELEANA upstream against the four-mile-per-hour current on the Detroit River. We finally arrived at Colony Marine around two o'clock that afternoon.

ELEANA was immediately moved to the lift well and then into the indoor service area. Within an hour, the service technician confirmed the prognosis that the transmission gears had been broken, and he immediately removed the transmission. Disassembly of the gear box disclosed that not just one of the eight gears had lost a tooth gear, but all the gears were broken. A single gear tooth had fallen into the mass of gears just at the right time to destroy the entire internal gearing system. The only alternative was to replace the entire starboard gear box.

We spent hours calling parts suppliers throughout the United States and Canada, and learned that only one starboard gear box existed, and it was in Fort Lauderdale, Florida. The sticker shock

> "In seven days we had completed one hundred miles of our 6,000-mile adventure. We wondered what the Lord had planned for the next 5,900 miles."

for the new gear box took my breath away, but we needed it—right away.

Transportation to St. Clair Shores by truck would take ten or more days. Air delivery would be three days. After discussion with Elaine, we agreed to have the gear box air freighted. While we waited for the gear box, Colony Marine obtained the generator parts and installed a new fuel filter. Fortunately for us, our daughter and son-in-law offered us transportation to and from Ann Arbor and a room while we waited.

Five days later, ELEANA was in the water, checked, and ready for us to resume our Great Loop cruise. The first seven days of our Great Loop adventure cost us ten thousand dollars, and we still had nine more months to go.

As we left the dealership and sped across Lake St. Clair toward the St. Clair River, we discussed our first week. We had completed one hundred miles of our six-thousand-mile adventure. We wondered what the Lord had planned for us during the next 5,900 miles.

Arriving in Port Huron, mentally preparing for entering Lake Huron, we were suddenly deluged by a severe thunderstorm with very high winds and a heavy rain. The seas were building from a north wind, reaching four to six feet. After battling the seas for ten miles, we tucked in at Lexington for the night.

Normally we didn't boat on Lake Huron or Lake Michigan this late in the summer, so we needed to be ready for fall storms. Stopping more often was to be expected.

The next morning, we departed at seven o'clock with seas at two to four feet. As the north wind increased, the seas were again building to four to six feet. With these conditions, it was necessary to slow down and take the waves on the bow. Quartering them at an angle, I was able to keep the propellers in the water. But Lake Huron was becoming very rough.

We began questioning why we needed to take this abuse, so we pulled into Port Sanilac for another night. Port Sanilac has a very nice restaurant, and thanks to the upcoming Labor Day weekend, it was open. They even sent a courtesy car to the marina to take and bring us back from dinner. We enjoyed a very special dinner and prayed we were going to be okay on the rest of the trip.

The next morning, the seas had settled to two to three feet as we headed north. Two hundred miles from Port Huron, we reached Presque Isle Marina.

And then we encountered our next challenge.

During my check of the engine compartment, I found fresh water in the bilge. How did this much rain water enter the bilge? Where could it have entered? A detailed flashlight review of the engine compartment provided no answers.

Elaine then mentioned that she had detected higher humidity in the aft stateroom, lounge, and kitchen area. The only way humidity would be high was if water was coming from our one-hundred-gallon freshwater tank, which was located under the aft stateroom bed.

Could it be a leaking hose connection?

I began to disassemble the aft stateroom to check out the L-shaped one-hundred-gallon freshwater tank set in a containment area, which had a leakproof wall surrounding it, so the tank wouldn't move when the boat was thrown about in rough seas. To my surprise, water was up to the top of the containment walls, totally covering the water tank.

I generally didn't keep the freshwater tank filled because the added weight slows the boat's speed and requires more fuel. Also, the marinas provide fresh water on the dock. However, at the start of this adventure, I had filled the tank in case the marinas' dock water systems on the Great Lakes had already been shut off for the winter.

A quick visual check revealed a crack in a corner of the water tank.

Our Great Circle trip of ten days ended at that moment! As in baseball, three strikes and we were out.

We sat down, tears flowing, giving thanks to the Lord that these things had happened in the first days of our Great Loop adventure and near home. We could only imagine if we had been in the hot south with leaking diesel fuel, a broken transmission, and a boat full of mold from the moisture of the broken water tank.

Upon our return home, the water tank was removed and ELEANA was placed in heated storage for the 2004-05 winter. As a follow-up to this story, Marine Max determined that the tank had been incorrectly designed. It relied on welded joints rather than a single molded piece of heavy polyethylene. Sea Ray provided a new, properly designed water tank free of charge.

Marine Max took out the containment walls and the flooring to expose the fiberglass inner hull. Since the water had been lying under the floor boards for an unknown of length time, it had gradually leached into the fiberglass hull. Trays of desiccant were emptied of water for the next six months before the hull was dry. We thanked the Lord that we had kept ELEANA in heated storage since we bought her in 1999.

Our ten-day venture took us a grand total of three hundred miles of our planned six-thousand-mile Great Loop Adventure in 2004. We never again considered taking the Great Loop. But we found another way to get away for the winter. We drove to the Florida Keys for the first three months of the new year and rented a fishing boat. Elaine enjoyed these tropical winters in the Keys so much that we continued winter getaways for the next ten years.

ELEANA continued to serve us for the next six years. In 2010, we sold her, and she went home to waters she had previously explored on Ontario's St. Lawrence River.

The memories will last forever! ■

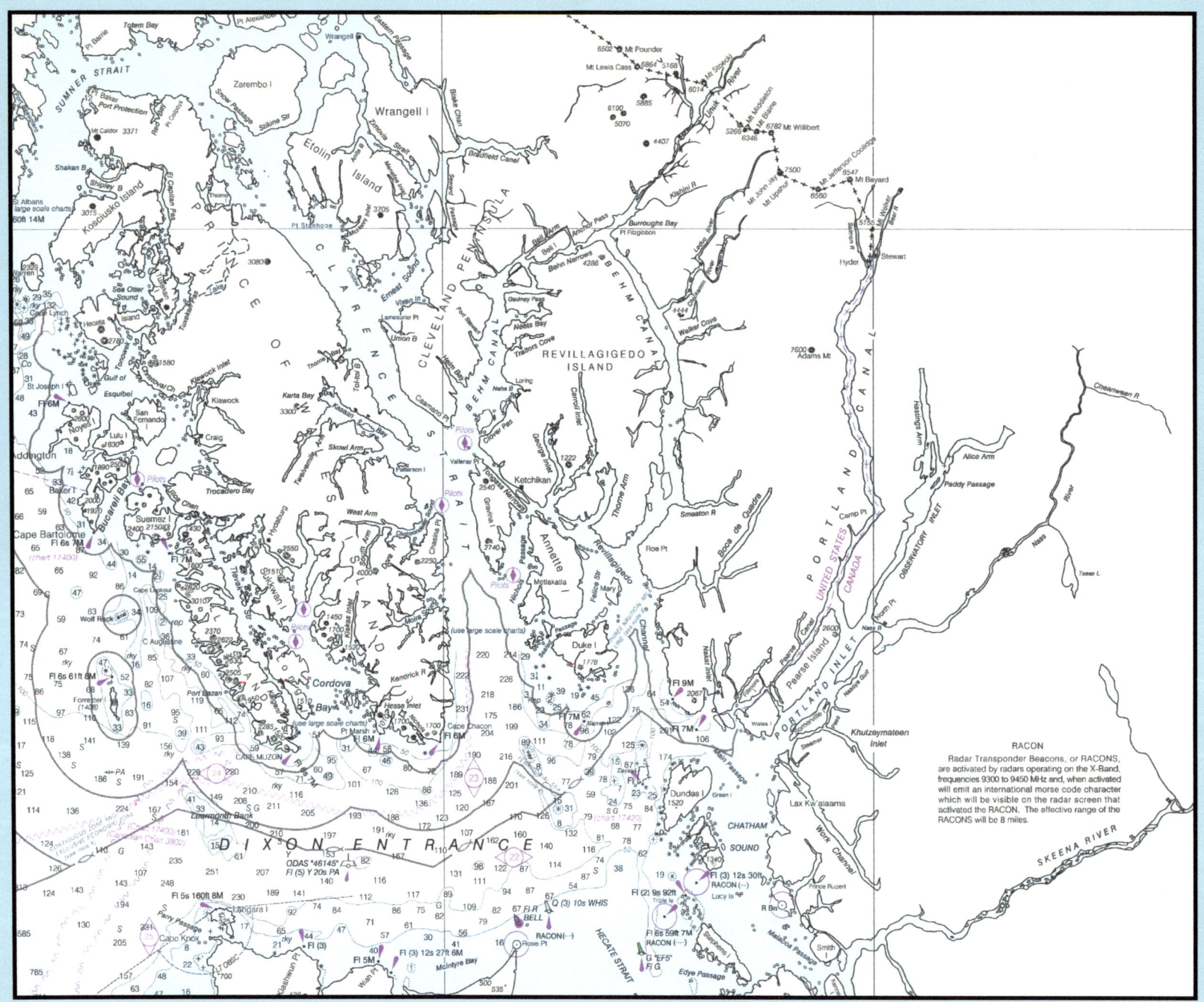

# CHAPTER 11
# Nine Days to Alaska

**DURING AN ENTIRELY NEW** training adventure in 2007, Elaine and I were at the helm of an Alaskan fishing vessel named the F/V AIMEE O, on our seventh of the nine-day training cruise, when we entered the Pacific's Dixon Entrance. Marking the border between Canada to the south and United States to the north, the entrance ushered us directly into the open waters of the Pacific Ocean. Sea swells were growing to ten feet high, but were far apart, so we had to work to stay on our designated course.

When the captain came forward, he ordered, "Increase our speed to at least ten to twelve knots. I just received an alert that a major storm is moving up the Pacific coast with heavy winds and forty-foot waves." He didn't ask to take the helm. Instead, he coached us as we increased speed and kept a straight course back to the protection of the Inner Passage.

Darkness had fallen as we approached within ten miles of the safety of the Inner Passage, and we began to observe the flashing lights of navigation beacons, something we had never experienced on the Great Lakes. Captain Steve asked Elaine to use our paper chart to locate each flashing beacon. I was able to make out the beacon on the radar and, of course, by the flash of light in my eyes.

Elaine called out the flash sequence for the port and starboard beacons, so I was able to pick out the towers on the radar. Working as a team, we entered the Inner Passage as if we knew what we were doing. Thankfully, we were ahead of the storm, although its flashes of lightning were clearly visible in the rear-view mirror.

Incidentally, we re-entered the United States during this crossing.

In the early fall of 2006, Elaine and I attended the Cedar Point Boat Show at Cedar Point Marina in Sandusky, Ohio. This yearly event offered me the opportunity to check out the latest technology, and it offered Elaine the opportunity to shop. A new exhibitor from Washington State caught my attention immediately. Evidently, Starpath specialized in radar software used for training Navy Personnel.

"Elaine, I have to find out more about this vendor," I announced, agreeing we'd meet at our normal lunch wagon.

I quickly found my way to the Starpath Company booth and met the manager of sales. As he demonstrated his software, I became intrigued. I had installed radar on my recent boats, but I had never been trained on how to use all of its capabilities. When I agreed to

> "I studied the new radar software program and realized I could definitely benefit from more training. My motto—*Be the Best!*—was ringing in my ears."

purchase the software, the manager described Starpath's onboard navigation courses and added, "The next course is set for April 2007, and it will be held on board a fishing boat called the F/V AIMEE O as it moves from the San Juan Islands of Washington to Sitka, Alaska for the 2007 salmon fishing season."

A class of six students would be on board for the nine-day leg departing from the San Juan Islands and heading to Ketchikan, he said. "The second class of six students will handle the five-day leg from Ketchikan to Sitka." Both legs would journey through the Inner Passage, with some distance in the open waters of the Pacific Ocean while the seasoned ship captain of the F/V AIMEE O would teach navigation skills using only radar and paper charts.

My attention was caught. I asked more questions and learned that each morning, three two-person teams would be announced by the captain, and they would be expected to spend time preparing for their two hours at the helm. Each day, all six students would have at least two hours of run time at the helm, and if desired, also could have six hours of experience on the bridge of the F/V AIMEE O. The rest of each day was available for sightseeing.

I told him I was very interested and would study the software and discuss this with my wife.

"Don't wait very long, as each leg only has six openings," was his response. To add to my growing interest, he explained that the F/V AIMEE O had three very nice two-person staterooms, three large bathrooms, and a galley that seats eight. A first mate would be on board to prepare meals, clean, wash clothes, and assist the captain.

I was sold on the course, the location, and the hands-on training. I hurried to meet Elaine for lunch, but I paid no attention to what I ate. "Hon, just think, all this training while on a private cruise ship!'

Elaine looked interested but unconvinced as she began opening bags and showing me her latest purchases. I had to comment, "You sure will look great in that outfit as we cruise the Inner Passage to Ketchikan!"

Later that day, I studied the radar software program and realized I could definitely benefit from more training. My motto—*Be the Best!*—was ringing in my ears. If there was a suddenly loss of chart input on my vessel, I always had paper charts ready, but I realized that I needed to know how radar would assist with navigation and keep all on board safe at all times and in all conditions.

"You'll have time at the helm, learning from someone other than me," I assured Elaine.

We decided this would be our 2007 cruise, and we signed up for the nine-day, 700-mile leg, from the San Juan Islands to Ketchikan. We made flight reservations to depart on April 9, 2007.

My brother Joe, a retired U. S. Navy Senior Master Chief with twenty-seven years of submarine underwater experience, lives with his wife Elaine in Port Townsend, Washington, close to the San Juan Islands. We flew into Seattle and took land transportation to Port

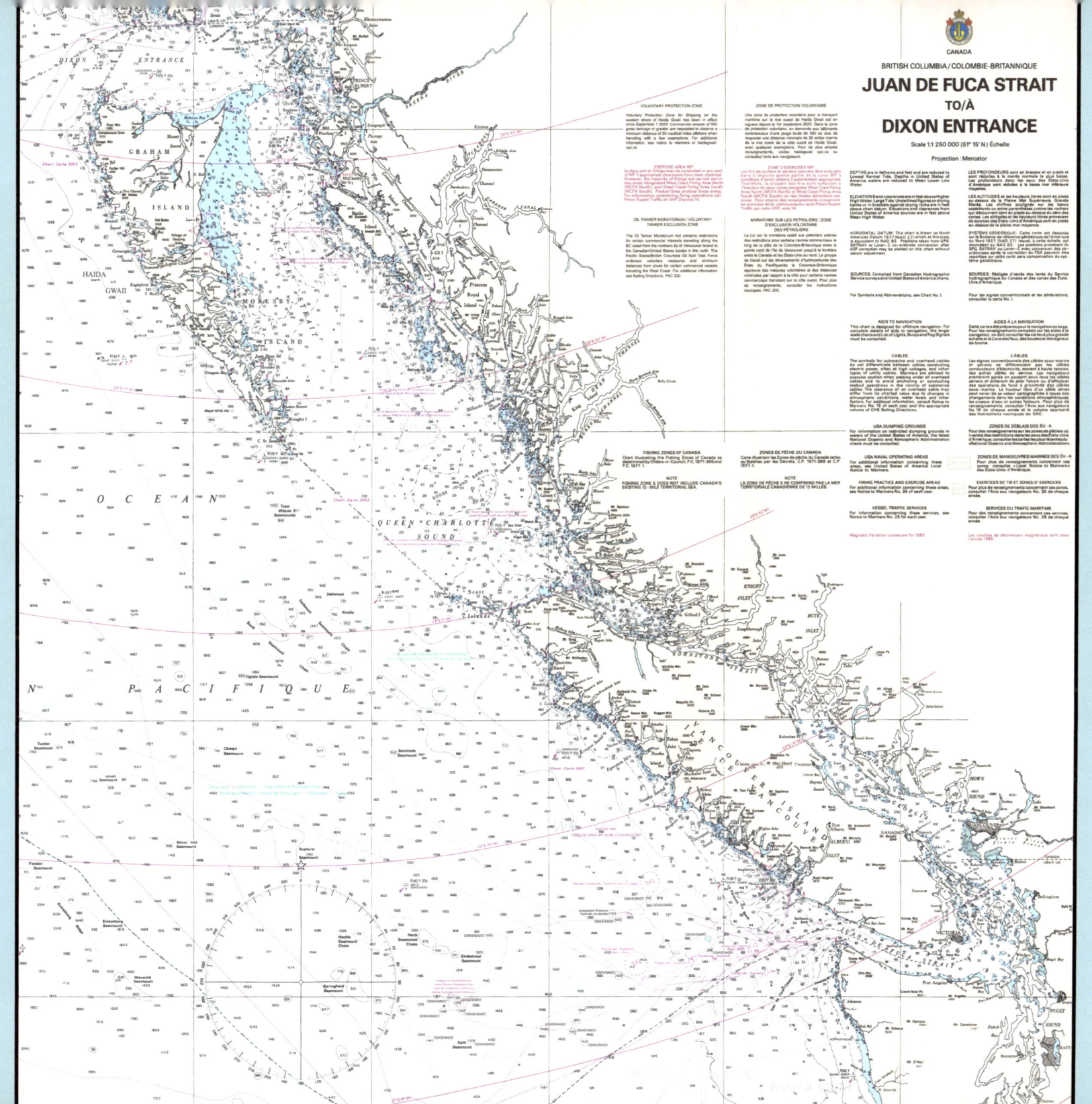

Townsend. On the day before F/V AIMEE O's planned departure, Joe and Elaine took us by ferry to Whitby Island, and then drove us to the San Juan Islands. We all stayed at a bed and breakfast for the night before Elaine and I boarded the F/V AIMEE O the next morning, April 9, 2007.

The AIMEE O is a steel vessel fifty-eight feet long, twenty-one feet wide, with a ten-foot draft. She is a seiner. A huge net is pulled out from her hold while small boats spread it out in a circle on the water. At the proper time, the huge net is pulled in by a vertical crane and lifted onto the deck of the vessel. The fish are then sorted and dropped into the water tank in her hull.

To prepare the vessel for holding the fresh-caught salmon, the vessel is first taken out on the Pacific Ocean to find the coldest salt water to fill the hull. The ship's cooling system maintains this water at thirty-three degrees. Two generators provide the energy for the cooling system and for all other electrical power needed on board.

*The AIMEE O is a 58-foot-long seiner, a fishing vessel that pulls a huge net out of its hold and spreads it in the water. In time, it lifts its catch of fish with a vertical crane, and then crew members sort the fish and store them in a water tank located in her hull.*

*Teams of two were stationed at the helm, using radar and charts to navigate the vessel from the San Juan islands to Ketchikan over the course of nine days.*

The F/V AIMEE O cruises at a speed of eight knots per hour with a single 500-hp Cummins N14 6-cylinder diesel. She carries eight thousand gallons of diesel, sufficient for the entire trip up, fishing, and returning to her home port in Washington State. She also carries 1,400 gallons of fresh water. We were told that in 2006, she harvested more than 600 tons of salmon.

Upon boarding the F/V AIMEE O, we chose a stateroom in what appeared to be a stainless steel building located on the aft deck of the seiner vessel. This unit contained two staterooms, two bathrooms, a complete kitchen, and an eating/seating area. The first mate, who was the daughter of the owner, explained that this building was designed to be lifted on and off the vessel and placed on the concrete slab at their property in Sitka. The fresh water, sewer, and electrical connections were designed into the unit so it would fit directly onto the same fittings that exist on the pad and on the F/V AIMEE O.

*Wildlife surrounded us on our adventure, including American eagles and a porpoise gliding off in the distance.*

We found the stateroom very comfortable and quiet. A husband and wife from San Francisco settled in the other stateroom. The F/V AIMEE O had a third stateroom within the main part of the vessel; two gentlemen were assigned there, one from Montana and the other from South Carolina.

We were then called together and introduced to Captain Steve, a thin, six-foot, gray-haired gentleman who had been captain of the vessel for many years. He and the first mate led us on a complete tour, with a special emphasis on safety and emergency procedures.

Captain Steve explained that our nine days and eight nights would take us through open and narrow channels of the Pacific Ocean. We would be dealing with twenty-four-foot tidal water-level changes (tidal change) twice every twenty-four hours. The tide change creates eight-knot tidal currents in some areas, and would mean we wouldn't even move forward if we attempted to go against the tide. On the Great Lakes, Elaine and I had only dealt with currents of this magnitude in certain rivers.

"I will personally do all of the docking, and I'll be overseeing all of the anchoring maneuvers you will have the opportunity to perform," he promised. "You're here to learn how to navigate using paper charts and radar. We have a chart plotter and satellite navigation on board, but only to use in case of an emergency."

During our voyage, we would be using 130 charts that were carefully maintained in sequential order and kept in a particular drawer. He pointed to the chart filing cabinet. "You must keep them in their numerical order, because they will be needed in case of an emergency."

He turned on the radar and showed its set-up. "You will not touch or change any settings without my permission, and only in my presence. When you are at the helm, I will be the only one to show or

*Porpoises raced the AIMEE O as we journeyed north to Ketchikan.*

*Captain Steve was an excellent teacher, determined that all his students would master the use of radar. Under his watchful eye, Elaine takes the helm.*

demonstrate the radar, and I will answer your questions—don't be afraid to ask questions!" He explained that when we were on helm duty, the engine room would be inspected every half hour and data taken according to a specific list of readings.

The first mate added, "Approaching or departing from a dock, each of you will be assigned specific duties and the location where you will be stationed. Listen carefully and execute them as defined. When we drop anchor for the night, I will identify who will assist me at the bow for dropping the anchor."

Captain Steve announced that each evening he would name the three two-person teams for the following day. They would be expected to spend time preparing for every two-hour shift at the helm.

After lunch, we left for Vancouver Island, where we would temporarily dock while we registered with Canadian Immigration and Customs in Sydney Harbor. When we arrived, Elaine was stationed at the bow with a large round fender, and I was at the stern with another large round fender in hand. The first mate told us where she wanted the fenders to be located as Captain Steve maneuvered the vessel smartly into a tight location.

In the Great Lakes, I had always tied off the fenders at specific locations. The first mate asked me to move the fender to two different locations as we docked, mainly using it as a safety fender if a problem occurred. I have since used this moving fender method many times when docking and undocking.

We temporarily tied off, and together Elaine and I entered the Immigration Office to register. The customs and immigration processes were straightforward, the same procedures we followed when going to Ontario.

Next, we moved to North Cove, directly across the Inner Passage from the city of Vancouver. The tide was changing and docking was more of a challenge, but the captain's skill was very evident as he used the reverse pull-to-port while skillfully moving the vessel into a tight dock location.

I don't recall what we ate for our first dinner on board, but I do recall the meal was fantastic. Our first mate was also a skilled chef. After dinner, we watched the sunset over the mountains of Vancouver Island. Totally exhausted, we finally decided to go to bed so we would be ready for the 5:20 wake-up call.

Elaine confessed, "Hon, I'm overwhelmed and nervous. I hope I can get a good night's sleep." But I was so excited to be on salt water with its tide changes and tidal currents that I hardly slept. When I did, I dreamed of what we would be doing and seeing in the next days.

When we awoke, our ship was at low tide. We wondered if we were in a different place, because we were twenty-four feet lower in relation to the surrounding landscape. Fenders were distributed and the captain again skillfully backed us out of the marina as the first mate gave orders where to place them.

After we were underway, we enjoyed a huge breakfast of eggs, bacon, and toast with plenty of black coffee. Neither Elaine nor I were on the first team at the helm, but we both stayed in the wheelhouse to observe and listen to everything the captain was saying. When he wasn't busy, I asked questions about the tide and tidal currents.

As we cruised at eight knots, porpoises swam along with us, eagles flew overhead, and we marveled at a whale pod swimming north in the distance. The Canadian Snowbirds, the Canadian flight group equal to America's Blue Angels, practiced their flight maneuvers above us.

In the late afternoon, Elaine and I were assigned to the helm. We had studied the charts relevant to our passage through the Seymour Narrows and identified all the markers for the rock shoals. While Elaine was on the helm, I studied the radar and called out the markers as we approached and passed the rocks. While riding the tidal current through the narrows, the captain called out "ten knots." Later, he

*The Pacific Ocean nearly touched our toes as we made our way to a seaside picnic on a chilly April day.*

*On our fifth day at sea, we rode the eight-knot tidal current through narrow and rocky channels.*

turned the vessel into a narrow cove in Granite Bay. Elaine and I were called to assist the first mate on the release of the anchor when the order from the bridge was given.

This was our first night on a hook. Granite Bay is very small, and the high ground around the bay created a well-protected area free from wind and currents. The sun had disappeared early, due to the high ground, and the April air was quickly turning cold. We bundled up with blankets as we watched the night sky turn into a sea of stars, which soon filled the entire sky. A night sky that we talked about for many years afterward.

The third day was routine. Elaine and I were on different teams, and this segment of the trip was much shorter. After an early arrival at Port Mitchell, we tied up to a marina dock and enjoyed a walk through the streets of the town. The largest port in the area, Port Michell is almost at the northern tip of Vancouver Island.

The fourth day was sunny with occasional clouds. We had smooth sailing, with seas less than one foot as we crossed the forty miles of ocean to Queen Charlotte Sound. Passing by Calvert Island, Captain Steve ordered the helm team to turn sharply to port into Pruth Bay. We cruised to the west end, where we dropped anchor.

Over the PA, he announced that we would lower the motorized dingy, which we would take to the west end of the bay. After walking one-quarter of a mile to the shore of the Pacific Ocean, we discovered, to our delight, that the first mate had prepared sandwiches and drinks so we could enjoy our lunch on the Pacific beach.

On the fifth day, Captain Steve announced that we would have the opportunity to ride the eight-knot tidal current through some extremely narrow and rocky channels.

When we arrived at a large pool of water, the captain called for the anchor team to drop anchor. "We'll wait here for about an hour for the tide to rise to its maximum height, and then we'll lift the anchor and ride the current through the rocky narrows, located right off the bow. I'll use the navigation system to record our speed during the ascent to open water. Everyone can be at the helm to watch as we reach top speed."

An hour later, we all gathered at the bridge while the anchor was lifted. The captain put the AIMEE O into gear to move the boat into the current. As we started down the chute between the rocks, we called off our speed in unison, until we reached fourteen knots (approximately sixteen miles per hour), when everyone cheered.

On day six we stopped at Klemtu, a First Nation village on Swindle Island, to fill our 1,400-gallon freshwater tank. The dock was adjacent to a salmon fish-processing company that is owned and operated by the village. The natives were farm-raising salmon in the cold Pacific Ocean water around the coves and between the near islands.

*The AIMEE O stopped at Klemtu, a First Nation village on Swindle Island, to fill our 1,400-gallon freshwater tank and tour an impressive fish-processing plant.*

> "When I was at the helm, I would ask my team partner to look forward and make certain we were staying in our desired channel, while I piloted the vessel using only radar."

Captain Steve knew the manager of the operation, who came to the F/V AIMEE O and offered a tour of their operation. All of us agreed enthusiastically, and when we arrived, we were given freshly laundered coveralls before entering the operations.

We watched as the fresh-caught salmon were loaded onto an outside conveyor that lifted them up to an outside cleaning station. They were washed as they entered the immaculate inner room for further processing. Cleaned again, each fish was weighed and sorted. Heavy cardboard cartons were layered with crushed ice, and workers laid the proper weight of fish on the ice. More ice covered the fish, a lid was automatically secured on top, and the container was automatically sealed.

The sealed boxes were forwarded through the wall and loaded directly into refrigerated overland trailers. As soon as they were full, the trailers were moved to a barge destined for the mainland. I estimated that each fish was sent to market within two hours from the net in the sea to the tractor trailer on the mainland.

After marveling at this process, Elaine and I strolled to a platform overlooking the whole operation and the village. We met a well-dressed elderly native gentleman who was walking by, and I asked him a question about the area. Fortunately, he spoke English and was quick to engage in a conversation. Looking to the south I asked if the beautifully painted building in the distance was the village's tribal lodge.

"Yes."

Pointing to the large canoe on the shore in front of the facility, I asked, "Is that the tribe's official canoe? It's beautiful."

Again, "Yes."

To keep the discussion going, I asked, "What trees do you use to make such a large canoe?"

Grinning, he said, "It's called a fiberglass tree." He immediately burst out laughing, and so did we.

After the AIMEE O was filled with fresh water, we were again underway, with a sunny sky, no wind, and smiles on our faces.

My daily routine was to spend time in the helm area, listening to the captain providing advice and directions to the team stationed there. When I was at the helm, I would ask my team partner to look forward and make certain we were staying in our desired channel, while I piloted the vessel using only radar. I enjoyed maneuvering through tight places while relying on technology under the watchful eye of the captain.

Nearing the end of the seventh day, after darkness fell, I was stationed at the helm when the captain announced, "We'll be dropping anchor for the night in Bullhead Cove, which is located off the Inner

*Ketchikan, known as "Alaska's First City" and the "Salmon Capital of the World," is perched on Revillagigedo Island, in the midst of dramatic natural scenery. A popular port of call for cruise ships touring the Inside Passage, we arrived just two weeks before its cruise season began.*

*As we cruised toward Ketchikan, we passed Misty Bay, which is well named, since it was covered in mist throughout April, when the snows melt and waters cascade down from the mountaintops. The scenery looked like a succession of beautiful paintings.*

Passage." Elaine kept me informed of the flashing light markers as I found the entrance on radar and we entered. It was now midnight.

Looking over my shoulder, the captain advised, "Find the center of the cove and prepare to drop anchor." Without any wind or current, this was an easy task when using the radar. He then then continued. "I want to know the depth, and I want you to define the tide change between now, midnight, and tomorrow morning at six a.m."

Definitely a new challenge. Checking the tide table next to the helm, I calculated that we would have a ten-foot lift, so I added this to the depth and calculated the swing of the vessel. Checking the distance to the nearest rocks, I gave him the amount of chain to release with the anchor. Surprising me, he said, "Well done." He then repeated the amount of chain for the first mate to release.

The anchor was dropped, and the captain complimented us on our actions, decisions, and abilities. That memorable experience made this endeavor come to life for me. It provided more experience than I could possibly obtain anywhere else. I knew that I was much better prepared to be a captain on the Great Lakes.

The next morning, I quickly dressed and went topside to observe where we were, secretly hoping the AIMEE O was not resting on rocks. I found we hadn't pulled the anchor loose or miscalculated the tidal change. All was as planned. I was so happy.

Elaine and I spent the next two days sightseeing on our way to Ketchikan, visiting Misty Fjords and Bell Island Hot Springs on the AIMEE O. We had booked three nights in Ketchikan and had plenty of time in the museums and shops. The entire town was preparing for the first cruise ships to arrive in two weeks. We met local people and enjoyed conversations in restaurants and bars, learning more about life in this part of Alaska. We looked, but didn't find any fiberglass trees.

The nine days of intense navigation with charts and radar were extremely productive, enjoyable, and educational. This experience, I knew, would definitely contribute to our goal of mastering the Great Lakes. ■

*A sense of satisfaction and peace descended with the dusk on our last night. Glassy waters. Breathtaking scenery. A challenge met and accomplished. That's how I remember our nine days on the AIMEE O.*

"As a born-and-bred engineer who loves to figure things out, the opportunity to master new technologies and operate new equipment was right up my alley."

# CHAPTER 12
# My Career as Delivery Captain, With Elaine as First Mate

**LATE IN THE 2003** Lake Erie boating season, the Treasure Cove's Marine Max dealership on Catawba Island offered me a delivery captain's position for large new yachts. If the company needed to move yacht inventory between the different Marine Max facilities, Elaine and I were assigned to the job.

Marine Max facilities are located on the eastern Atlantic seaboard and the Great Lakes, and special dealerships provide sales and service in Minnesota and the Upper Mississippi River. When customers were considering the purchase of a new yacht, my assignment was to assist the sales person in discussing and demonstrating all the new vessel's components, features, technology, and operations. Often the yacht was a major upgrade in size and technology for the potential customer, so this process was critically important. The customer needed to realize the new vessel's capability and challenges.

Once a purchase was finalized, I often accompanied the owners as they motored their new boat to their private dock. During this trip, I demonstrated the navigation technology and equipment and then watched and answered questions as the owners operated the equipment for the first time.

When we arrived at their dock, I demonstrated the process of maneuvering the boat into its place, and I supervised them as they repeated the steps. On larger vessels, this familiarization process could take a number of days, sometimes even a week or more of follow-up.

As the final step, I took the captain into the engine compartment, described all of the equipment, and demonstrated the fluid level checks for all devices.

I also created and presented classes to acquaint spouses with the rules of the road and the operation of their new vessel, so they could handle it in case of an emergency. The majority of these students were women, only a few of whom were captains of their recently purchased boats.

After completing the class, each spouse was assigned to a vessel similar to the one they had purchased, and they began actual on-water training. Each took the helm and learned to dock the boat. I can't recall any spouse who wasn't successful by the end of the class, since they were serious about developing the skills to operate their vessel safely. I ended the class when I was convinced that they had

> "Elaine was an excellent first mate, thanks to our extensive experiences in cruising all of the Great Lakes, inland waters, and oceans."

the ability to pilot a boat in case of emergency. If they felt they needed additional experience, they were encouraged to sign up for private lessons.

As a born-and-bred engineer who loves to figure things out, the opportunity to master new technologies and operate new equipment was right up my alley. To keep pace with the latest mechanical, electrical, and navigational technology, I attended as many product-line seminars as possible.

When customers or dealerships required electronic upgrades, I installed the software. Depending on the level of the upgrade, I often taught the owners how to use the new technology. Often this required me to travel to the owners' private docks or marinas throughout the sales area, which stretched from Lake Erie to Lake St. Clair, and southern Lake Huron.

Staying attuned to the latest boating technology meant that Elaine and I needed to attend the famous annual Miami International Boat Show every February, as well as the annual Fort Lauderdale International Boat Show in the fall. At these single locations, we could observe all the latest boating innovations on the market in one place and watch demonstrations of the new technology. The shows' locations were an added bonus: Elaine and I enjoyed vacationing in southern Florida.

Elaine was an excellent first mate, thanks to our extensive experiences in cruising all of the Great Lakes, inland waters, and oceans. We had developed a unique way of communication, knowing and anticipating what each other needed or desired. We both knew what was required to motor successfully and safely on the water with all the various types and sizes of vessels—not to mention weather conditions. Elaine, with her keen eye, mastered skills necessary to keep the vessel on the desired course. She knew when and how to throw lines, drop fenders, tie-off vessels, scout for floating dangers, and anticipate whatever was needed, followed by an instantaneous response.

Marine Max had two dealerships on Lake Erie and a number along the Atlantic Coast. Its main operations were located on the west and east coasts of Florida, but there were others that stretched from the north coast of the Gulf to Alabama. If a dealership had a vessel in inventory matching what a customer wanted at another location, the customer generally traveled to see the vessel, although, in some cases, the boat would be moved to the customer's local dealership.

In these years, the price of fuel made vessel movement by water very practical, which meant that delivery captains were in demand. Early in the boating season, the states' weight restrictions on roads often required moving boats by water.

Because today's cost of fuel is so high, moving boats by truck is often more economical, but in my opinion, those heavy loads are responsible for damaging our roads. Also, when boats are moved cross-country by trucks, they often require disassembly and reassembly, based on their weight, the road width, and height restrictions. This means of transport can create more problems than if the vessel is delivered as originally manufactured.

Moving a large, completely finished boat by water requires no disassembly and reassembly. During the delivery voyage, any original discrepancies and problems can be identified and corrected before the boat is even shown to the customer. There is nothing like a shakedown cruise to determine if anything must be fixed.

The transfer by water was exactly what Elaine and I were capable of providing. Our employers recognized our extensive personal experiences, and we were ready for the challenges as we entered this new and exciting career.

Although the delivery of new boats was the job for which we were hired, we quickly began to assist Marine Max in their sales and service business. Our years of experience with our own water craft meant that we could identify and document problems as we operated the boat in different weather conditions and with different operational challenges. The sales team began taking our notes and observations to management, requesting that the quality and performance information we observed be corrected before the vessel was sold.

In one of many cases, when we were spending three winter months in the Florida Keys, we traveled to the Sea Ray factory on Merritt Island to inspect a 52 Sea Ray Sedan Bridge vessel under construction for an Ohio customer. After a detailed inspection, we made a list of issues requiring corrections prior to delivering the vessel to Ohio. Our list made some boat-building employees unhappy, but in the end, we were praised by the dealership and customer for identifying and fixing potential problems.

We knew the critical importance of having all the equipment and technology onboard ship-shape and operating at its fullest capability, and our goal was to help other boaters enjoy the same level of success. ■

*The AIMEE O Alaskan training voyage prepared us for our new venture.*

This $900,000 42 Sea Ray Sedan Bridge faced rough seas and high adventures on its maiden voyage from Ohio to Delaware.

# CHAPTER 13
# A Calamitous New Jersey Delivery

**THE START DATE** was set, Elaine and I had joined our client, his wife, and son on their new boat, ready to begin a twelve-day voyage from Ohio to Delaware. But the weather was terrible. Northeast winds were whipping Lake Erie waves from six feet to as much as eight feet.

After studying the conditions, I announced we were delaying the trip, but the boat owner who had hired Elaine and me to sail his $900,000 purchase insisted we had to meet his schedule. "We have to leave today!"

It was apparent he had little idea of what to expect in this weather. Our marina on Lake Erie is well protected by its islands, so I imagine he thought I was just trying to delay the trip.

"If you insist," I said.

Elaine and I put on our inflatable life jackets. I told the forty-something-year-old couple and their twelve-year-old son to do the same, but the owner refused. Elaine looked at me in horror, but I whispered, "He will have to learn to listen. And it starts now."

Departing on what the owner thought was our journey East, I maintained our path on the lee side of Kelleys Island. This approach kept us safe from the fury of Lake Erie until we turned to go around the island. Then, I knew, we would be confronted with the full force of the nor'easter blowing that day.

As I expected, when we turned the corner to head into the heavy seas, we encountered not only eight-foot waves, but strong winds spraying water off the wave tops. I quartered the first waves.

Almost immediately, a rogue wave crashed over the bow. The owners' stateroom hatch flew open, and buckets of water drenched the inside. The family screamed and panicked. I immediately began the difficult turn necessary to head back. We rolled quite hard to starboard.

Finally returning to the lee side of Kelleys Island, I called Marine Max and requested someone to vacuum up the water in the front stateroom. With calm authority, I told Dan, "If you want us to move your boat to Delaware, you have to listen to me! It's your decision."

At the end of July 2004, a couple and their teen-aged son arrived at the Treasure Cove Marine Max dealership in Ohio to view a 42 Sea Ray Sedan Bridge boat in our stock. They liked what they saw.

The Marine Max manager, Tom, called me and reported, "Pat, the couple from Delaware has purchased the $900,000 42 Sea Ray—on the condition that the boat be delivered to their dock on the Chesapeake and Delaware Canal. Also, they insist on riding along on the trip."

He continued, "Will you and Elaine be the delivery team? They're new to boating, and this is their first boat. They would never be able to navigate the Welland, Erie Barge Canal, and Hudson River."

Elaine and I had just planned our summer cruise on the Great Lakes, but I thought this opportunity would be a much nicer getaway—and we would be paid to do it. I asked for a moment to consult with

# "Dan went ballistic. 'I spent hundreds of thousands of dollars for this boat, and I want nothing but original parts!'"

Elaine, set the phone down, and found her outside. After quickly outlining the proposal, Elaine asked, "What size boat will we be traveling on, and who's going?" We took a few minutes to debate the plan, but when I returned inside, I told Tom we would do it.

The following day, Tom called again, asking us to take care of the family for the next couple of days while Marine Max prepared the boat for the customers' final approval. "They don't want to rent a car, and they're going to stay on board the boat."

Another new experience for Elaine and me.

We met the family and informed them we would be in charge of moving their vessel to Delaware. In the meantime, we offered to assist them while they waited for the boat to be prepared. For the sake of their privacy, I'll call the owners Dan and Sue, and their son, Jack.

It was late afternoon, and Sue asked if we could drive them to the grocery store. We immediately responded. "We're happy to take you."

We waited outside the grocery store and chauffeured them back to the boat. Upon exiting the car, Sue asked if we would join them for dinner. "You're welcome to choose the restaurant," she added.

It so happened that our Elks Club was sponsoring a special Lake Erie perch dinner, and Elaine asked if they were interested. Jack immediately said he didn't like fish, but I listed other menu items, and the family agreed our choice would be fine with them.

The opportunity to get acquainted with someone new before spending twelve days together on a confining boat sounded like a great idea. Everything was going well until Sue more or less forced Jack to eat a fillet of perch. Jack took several bites and started choking.

Without going into the gory details, we ended up taking him to the hospital emergency room to extract a fish bone from Jack's mouth. But neither a nurse nor a doctor could do anything about a tiny fish bone lodged in Jack's throat, so we returned the family to their boat. I tried to convince Jack that eating a large center of bread would take the bone down, but it was impossible to get Jack to try. A harbinger of things to come.

I began preparing for the trip by verifying the vessel's vertical dimensions, ensuring it would clear obstructions, roads, and railroads on the Oswego and Erie Barge Canals.

We would cruise the length of Lake Erie, enter Canada, and pass through the Welland Canal to Lake Ontario. Then the voyage would take us the length of Lake Ontario before we returned to the U.S.A. in Oswego, New York. I verified the fact that the family had their passports.

To reach the Erie Barge Canal, we would motor up the Oswego River's seven locks to the canal, then follow the canal on its eastward journey through twenty-three locks before we would finally enter the Hudson River. After navigating to New York's Harbor, we'd head south on the Atlantic Ocean, following the coastline along the New Jersey East shore to Delaware Bay.

I estimated the trip would take us nine or ten days to New York Harbor and another two days to their marina.

This was going to be our first cruise with a family on board.

As we returned to the marina after our first attempt to depart, I told the family, "Based on the present forecast, we might be able to start in two days. We'll get underway as soon as the weather forecast is acceptable. I'll keep you informed."

*I verified the boat's dimensions, ensuring it would clear obstructions, roads, and railroad crossings as we proceeded from Lake Erie through the Welland Canal, Oswago River, Erie Barge Canal, Hudson River, New York Harbor, New Jersey coastline, and the Delaware Bay.*

Two days later, we were underway. Waves were two to four feet high, and the trip was uneventful. When we reached Erie, Pennsylvania, we were able to obtain a dock at the Erie Yacht Club, where we enjoyed a delicious dinner together. Tensions were reduced.

During my morning engine room check, I noticed a pinkish stain under the starboard engine. Using my flashlight, I was unable to locate where it was coming from. I knew I had to keep checking.

The next morning, we were underway early, with seas down to one to two feet. The day was beautiful and sunny as we cruised to Port Colborne, Ontario, and into the entrance into the Welland Canal. I explained how the Welland locks would lower us the 326 feet to Lake Ontario.

About halfway to Port Colborne, I asked Dan to take the helm, as I wanted to check the engine room. As soon as I entered, I saw diesel fuel under the starboard engine. I grabbed the fuel diapers I always kept handy, and placed them to absorb the fuel.

Searching for the source, I found the hose carrying fuel to the starboard engine was leaking at the connection where the flexible hose met the metal connector. The amount of fuel in the bilge wasn't significant enough to necessitate shutting the engine off, but I was now going to have to keep collecting the leaked fuel. After arranging for pails and diapers in the immediate area, I went topside to inform Dan of the situation.

Attempting to avoid a panic, I summarized what we would need when we reached Port Colborne. The starboard fuel line was leaking due to a faulty connection in the hose, but I would be able to absorb the leaked fuel and safely store it in my containers. We would have to obtain a new hose upon our arrival in Port Colborne.

*Our "trip from hell" included traversing the Oswago River at flood stage.*

Dan immediately rushed to the engine compartment, while Sue screamed and cried. I called Marlon Marina in Port Colborne, asking for a technician to be waiting for us on the dock when we pulled in at about 9:30 am. When we docked, the family and Elaine checked in with Canadian Customs and Boarder Control while the technician removed the hose and left.

He returned to say there wasn't a spare part for the Cummins engine in the area.

Dan went ballistic. "I spent hundreds of thousands of dollars for this boat, and I want nothing but original parts!"

Calmly, I pointed out, "You are now in Canada, and if the vessel can't move until a Cummins part is on it, I suggest you begin your journey to America to find one. George says he can have a new part made, and he'll install it tonight. You can keep the original and have it replaced when you get home."

Dan had to agree. By one o'clock in the afternoon, the hose was installed, and I called Welland to obtain permission to move to the queuing area.

We waited for two and a half hours before we were called to begin our descent. As we were proceeding through the lock system, I called Port Dalhousie Marina for a dock number, as I knew they would be closed by the time we arrived—which I estimated would be around midnight.

I highly encouraged—forced, actually—Dan and Sue to man the bow and stern following Elaine's instructions while I stayed at the helm. She was an excellent taskmaster, insisting on perfection. I was so proud of her.

The following morning, we departed from Port Dalhousie on our way to Oswego. There we would clear U.S. Customs and Immigration, fuel, and travel up the Oswego River's seven locks to the Erie Barge Canal. I had made a reservation in Brewerton for our next overnight.

At one o'clock, when I was fueling the boat, the family asked to go shopping in Oswego. "Be back by 3:30 p.m.," I said firmly. "Our reservation is only good to midnight. If we don't arrive by then, we won't have a place to tie up for the night."

At 4:30, I went into town to search for them. To no avail. They finally returned at 5:30, apologizing and saying they had lost track of time. I knew we had to push very hard to reach the marina by midnight. We certainly would have to eat dinner on the way.

We immediately started up the Oswego River, which, incidentally, was at flood stage. We transversed the seven locks and arrived at the Erie Barge Canal 10:30 p.m.

Finding the Erie Barge water very high and filled with debris, I continued on our way, avoiding the large branches. But Dan was on the bow pointing and looking back, worried about small debris, trying to get me to change direction. As I pushed to make up for the lost time, I continued to say, "We have to arrive before midnight, or we'll have to drop anchor in Lake Oneida for the night. I'm not going to let that happen."

We reached Ess-Kay Yards in Brewerton, New York, at 11:45 p.m., just before Kim and Ethan closed at midnight.

I recall telling Elaine, as we prepared for bed that night, "This has turned out to be a trip from or to hell—or both."

After an early start the next morning, we began by crossing Lake Oneida. When we reentered the Erie Canal, we were lucky

*We felt a sigh of relief when we reached the Statue of Liberty--only to be told that we had to take sanctuary in her parking lot, due to a bomb threat.*

A CALAMITOUS NEW JERSEY DELIVERY

*The final straw that broke the boat buyers' resolve occurred when the U.S. Coast Guard, armed with machine guns, arrived to tell us that we had to evacuate the boat due to a bomb scare. Within a half hour, our passengers fled the scene.*

to find the canal wasn't busy. We were able to push and reach our normal stop at the Riverside Park in Canajoharie. After docking, we all walked downtown to our favorite Italian Restaurant, where everyone enjoyed a fantastic dinner. No fish bones.

The following day, we reached the Hudson River and followed it down to the Troy Downtown Marina fuel dock. I had called the harbormaster in advance, and he confirmed that he would hold a spot for us at the fuel dock, so we could make an early morning departure. After fueling, we walked to our favorite local Troy restaurant.

Before entering the Atlantic, our normal stop for fuel was at Liberty Landing Marina, located on the New Jersey side of New York Harbor, between the Statue of Liberty and Jersey City. We planned to arrive that night. But, while topping off the fuel, I checked the weather and learned that tropical storm Alex was moving up the New Jersey coast. Thunderstorms and heavy seas were reported south of the Manasquan Inlet, the first inlet—and it was fifty miles south of our current location.

My plan had been to fuel and continue on the Atlantic Ocean to Delaware Bay at Cape May, 150 miles south of our current location. I decided not to take a chance. I didn't want us caught on the ocean in what appeared to be a serious storm. I informed the family that we needed to stay overnight at Liberty Landing and evaluate the weather again in the morning.

More grumbling.

Our dock assignment was situated in the last open back-corner slip, against a walkway to the fuel dock. This location forced me to turn the boat around and back it down the channel into the assigned slip. I was able to find a spot to turn around, with the anchor bow pulpit moving over the stern of one boat, while our swim platform slid under the bow pulpit of the boat to the rear. As I was making this maneuver, Dan and Sue were yelling directions at me. As if they knew what I should be doing.

After making the turn without any issues, I successfully backed into the slip without touching anything, and Elaine tied us off. Sue was crying, evidently terrified that their new boat would be scratched or worse. For me, it was just a normal maneuver.

We were all relaxing when I noticed three U.S. Coast Guard boats entering the main channel into the Liberty Landing Marina. Each was manned with machine guns on the bow and stern. I jumped to the dock and ran down to the fuel dock to ask what was happening. Officers informed me that the high-rise Jersey City building next to the water entrance into Liberty Landing was under a bomb threat. They recommended we leave our boat and the marina, and walk into the Statute of Liberty parking lot. We would be advised when to return to the boat.

The date was August 1, 2004, nearly three years after 9/11. Sue began having another meltdown, and, I assumed, reliving the 9/11 tragedy. Within thirty minutes, the family informed me they were leaving and going home. "We can't take it anymore! This trip has been so stressful," Sue blurted out, with tears streaming down her cheeks.

Shortly afterwards, a cab arrived. Without a goodbye or "thank you," they were gone.

Elaine and I celebrated with the fantastic wine and wonderful food left on board from their lengthy shopping expedition. Now, at least, we appreciated the fact they had purchased so much food in Oswego.

The storm was projected to last for three or four days, so I spoke to the Marine Max in Bear, Delaware and another in Brick, New Jersey. I reluctantly said we would attempt to enter the Manasquan Inlet and take the boat to the Brick facility the next day, weather permitting. They could then deliver it to the owner's dock in the Chesapeake-Delaware Canal when the weather cleared.

The following morning, the storm had slowed on its northern path, so we entered the Atlantic Ocean, fighting eight-to-ten-foot seas. According to the latest weather report, the storm had already neared the entrance into Manasquan Inlet. We were dealing with a slow, rough ride, but we were anxious to finish this delivery.

We knew that the northbound wind and waves would definitely be creating shoaling within the Manasquan Inlet. Since we were not familiar with the inlet, my worry became more intense as we slowly moved toward the entrance.

Fortunately, as we approached, three large, seventy-foot fishing boats were returning from the south, racing ahead of the major incoming storm. I decided to hold a position outside the entrance and follow them in. Their vessels had much deeper drafts, and most likely, their captains would know where shoaling would occur.

Once the fishing boats entered the channel, I tucked in behind them and carefully followed. They made a couple of turns, indicating to me the channel was shoaling.

After we docked at Marine Max in Brick, New Jersey, the manager drove us to a Hertz office to rent a car.

Words cannot describe how happy we were to be driving home. That nine-day trip tested our patience and fortitude. It was filled with episodes of great frustration. We were thankful to the Lord for giving us the patience and perseverance to complete the job.

This was one of the most stressful deliveries we ever made, but not the last. In later years, we wondered whether Dan, Sue, and Jack ever climbed aboard their boat again. ∎

## "Words cannot describe how happy we were to be driving home."

*What was supposed to be a routine six-day spring cruise on a $1.4 million boat turned out to be a series of adventures laced with mechanical difficulties.*

## CHAPTER 14
# 600 Sea Ray Sun Sport Challenge

**"I'VE LOST CONTOL!"**

What was supposed to be a last-minute pick-up of a new sixty-foot Go Faster Sea Ray Sun Sport, priced at $1.4 million, had just turned into a nightmare in Lock 7 of the Canadian Welland Canal.

The twenty-five-ton boat had suddenly and violently been raised two or more feet on a mountain of incoming water, and then it immediately slid sideways off this mountain of water toward the lock's north wall. If we didn't stop the slide, we would slam into the cement wall, potentially sinking the boat and killing Elaine and our helper, Dan, as well as me. Those thoughts flashed through my brain.

On this day in early spring, I was reminded that even with the desire and drive to be the best captain on the Great Lakes, there will always be tests of one's instincts and responses.

This adventure started with a phone call and simple request very early in May of 2004. Steve, the manager of Marine Max Catawba, explained that a captain and first mate had piloted a new 600 Sea Ray Sun Sport from a Marine Max facility in Florida as far as Oswego, New York. Their mission was to deliver the 600 SS to Cleveland and return to Florida with the new 480 Sea Ray Sedan Bridge presently on Catawba. But the generator of the 600 SS had stopped running while they were on the Erie Barge Canal, and when they attempted to continue across Lake Ontario, the port engine refused to exceed 1,500 rpm.

"They were unable to find anyone to repair the diesel engine, and they are freezing, since the generator isn't working and the marina hasn't turned on electrical power," Steve told me, adding that evidently the Floridian captain and first mate had also failed to bring warm clothes to Michigan in early spring. They only had shorts and shirts to wear.

"Captain Pat," Steve continued, "in addition, Florida needs the 480 as soon as possible. Would you and Elaine take the 480 to Oswego and trade it for the Sun Sport? And can you leave in the morning?" He was speaking in a pleasant "help me" voice.

I turned to Elaine. "Hey, Hon, would you like to take a couple days' break and head to Lake Ontario? It sounds like fun!" Before she could answer, I added, "We leave early tomorrow morning."

The 480 Sea Ray SB had recently been delivered to Catawba by truck, so I wanted to be certain it was fit to make its first major voyage. That afternoon, I went on board to inspect all systems, and activate them, to be certain everything worked properly. I inspected all twenty or more fluid levels and started engines, checking to ensure all were in working order.

Since we were passing through Canada, Marine Max prepared the required vessel documentation.

> "As we checked in for the overnight stay at the marina, we were notified we were the first visitors at Port Dalhousie for the 2004 boating season."

I turned on all the navigation equipment to be sure it was functioning properly, and I loaded the specific navigation data needed for the trip. We were boarding a new boat, worth more than one million dollars, that hadn't been thoroughly checked. It was like leaving for a five-hundred-mile trip with a brand new car that had just been delivered to the dealership.

My years of determination to be the best captain on the Great Lakes would again be tested. I was confident that I was the right captain for this job, particularly since I had the best first mate in the business. The Marine Max request wasn't unusual during the years since I obtained my captain's license, but it came very early in the boating season. The Marine Max Catawba motto seemed to be, "Give the tough deliveries to Captain Pat and First Mate Elaine."

Unlike a pilot preparing for a flight with a planned route and traffic controller guiding him around weather and traffic, the captain on the water is the all-in-one person. First, planning the route, and then, when underway, checking the weather, standing on watch for logs, debris, and fish nets that radar can't pick up on a ship's radar screen.

The next morning, we boarded the 480 Sea Ray Sedan Bridge for the planned seven o'clock departure. Although I had made a list of the equipment to be on board, the staff hadn't even begun to collect it. While waiting for that to happen, we brought our carry-on bags on board, plus our inflatable life jackets, clothes, bedding, toiletries, toilet paper, coffee, food, garbage bags, paper charts, hand-held backup electronic devices, and our normal safety gear for this extended round trip.

During my routine re-inspection of the vessel, I discovered that the generator wouldn't start. We needed the generator to power the heat pump, since the Lake Erie water temperature was thirty-nine degrees at this time of year and the air temperature wasn't much higher. The forecast report for Lake Ontario, which is farther north, was also thirty-nine degrees. A technician corrected the problem, which hadn't occurred the previous day.

I wondered if we had packed enough warm clothes.

After inspecting to make sure all of my requested equipment and items were on board, we finally got underway at 7:35 that morning. With the seas at less than one foot, we were comfortably running at 27 knots (between 31 and 32 miles per hour), so we anticipated arriving in Port Colborne in plenty of time for dinner. We planned a pass-through on the Welland Canal first thing the next day.

At three o'clock, we arrived at Marlon Marina in Port Colborne, located just outside the entrance to the Welland Canal. I called and registered us with Canadian Immigration and Customs, filled the diesel tanks, and calibrated some of the navigation electronics. I then called Dan, our preferred helper, to ask if he was available the following day to assist us. He said he was. This highly experienced young man was a college student we used exclusively over the years.

Little did we know how much we would need him in the future.

*We were boarding a new boat, worth more than one million dollars, that hadn't been thoroughly checked. Immediately we learned the generator wouldn't start. And that was the beginning of our ordeal, which also included freezing temperatures, thick fog, mechanical failures, and marinas without fuel.*

The next morning, we met Dan at the Welland Canal queue area at seven o'clock. We called in and were directed to begin our 326-foot descent to Lake Ontario immediately. I had anticipated that we would be the only pleasure craft in the canal this early in the boating season.

We quickly traversed Locks 8 through 2, but had to tie off before Lock 1 while we waited for a down-bound freighter to be lowered and an up-bound freighter lifted through that lock before we could enter. When we finally cleared Lock 1, we were at Lake Ontario water level.

As we checked in for the overnight stay at the marina, we were notified we were the first visitors at Port Dalhousie for the 2004 boating season. We passed through Port Weller into Lake Ontario and arrived in Port Dalhousie's marina at three o'clock in the afternoon, where Dan left the boat. We were exhausted after the nine-hour trip through the Welland, and we called for a taxi to take us into town to have a relaxing dinner.

The following morning, our third day, we departed on the 140-mile cruise across Lake Ontario. The waves were only one foot, but the thirty-nine-degree water temperature made it a very cold day. The trip was uneventful and comfortable, with the generator running the onboard heat pump.

We arrived at Oswego Marina at 1:15 that afternoon, and made an attempt to fuel the 480 for the trip to Florida, but the harbormaster told us they didn't have diesel fuel, that it was too early in the boating season. I explained our need for fuel, not only the 480, but also to fill the 600 SS for our return trip.

"Can you call for a diesel fuel truck to come and fill both vessels?" I asked, suggesting that we could potentially need about 1,500 gallons. Fortunately, the harbormaster was able to find a source that would provide diesel for both vessels in the morning.

We moved off the fuel dock and tied off next to the 600 SS. I called the Florida captain to inform him that we had arrived and I had ordered fuel to be delivered tomorrow. The captain and mate had moved to a nearby motel since there was no heat onboard the 600 SS.

The next morning, we fueled both vessels. Elaine and I transferred our gear and personal possessions from the 480 onto the 600 SS, and in the early morning, Captain Charlie and his first mate departed, on their way to Florida with the 480 SB.

As soon as Elaine descended into the galley, she called up to me, "You can't imagine the mess in the eating area. Dirty dishes, garbage everywhere, It's hardly fit for human habitation!" The only saving grace was that the forward stateroom and head hadn't been used.

I immediately began my inspection, and we started a written log of problems we noted on this brand-new 600 Sun Spot Sea Ray. Before starting our return, I wanted to be certain that all systems were fit for the return journey of five hundred miles.

The generator had stopped working somewhere on the trip from Florida, so we wouldn't have any heat unless we were able to get the generator running. Unfortunately, I didn't find any manuals or instructions for any of the equipment on the boat. This wasn't what I would expect from anyone delivering a $1.4 million new boat!

I decided to take the 600 SS out onto Lake Ontario to determine what was wrong with the port MAN diesel engine. Clearing the city break-wall, I powered up the twin 1,300-horsepower engines, only to discover that the port engine would only go to 1,500 rpm. If I synchronized the port and starboard engines at 1,500 rpm, we could only attain a forward speed of less than ten mph. A definite no-go situation. As I recall, the optimum rpm of the twin 1,300 hp MANs was about 2,200 rpm, and this would drive the boat at more than forty mph.

We needed technical assistance.

The Oswego harbormaster informed us there were no diesel technicians in the area this early in the boating season. In prior years, we had traversed the Erie Barge Canal and regularly stayed at Ess-Kay Yards in Brewerton, New York, managed by Kim and Ethan. They always provided diesel support and told us they were available should we ever need help. Now was the time to call on them.

According to a local road map, their operation in Brewerton was only twenty-five miles by car from our location, but much longer by boat on the Oswego and Erie Barge Canals. When we called, Ethan promised to send his diesel technician, who arrived at 4:30 that afternoon. Craig worked for three hours. First, he discovered that the port and starboard engine fuel filters needed to be replaced.

The night before, we had discussed what might be required, so he had brought new Raycor fuel filters with him and installed them immediately. However, the Raycor filter he brought for the generator was not correct. He said he would try to get one. So, oh happy day, we were destined for another cold night.

We took the 600 SS out to check if the fuel filters were the only problem. Upon exiting the harbor for the test run, we were immediately stopped and boarded by five U.S. Coast Guard Coasties for a vessel inspection. I guessed we were their first pleasure craft seen for the 2004 boating season—and this was a beautiful, super-rare boat on Lake Ontario. I guessed they had to check it out so they would have something to talk about.

The situation became stressful and irritating, since Florida Marine Max had not provided sufficient ownership documentation to identify the vessel. In addition, Craig became very upset and vocal when they refused to let him work on the engines. He was directed to sit next to Elaine. The stress caused everyone to become impatient. Tensions grew.

To try and de-escalate the tension, I phoned Marine Max on Catawba and turned the phone over to the Coastie in charge of the crew. Finally, after more than an hour, we were released. We slowly returned to Oswego Marina knowing the new fuel filters hadn't solved the port engine problem.

Craig and I agreed the problem wasn't with the port engine software. The port code was now "coolant pressure water pump." Neither he nor I knew what that meant. Craig said he would check with MAN's technical department as soon as he returned to Brewerton.

As we gathered clothes, towels, and anything on board to keep us warm for the night, Elaine asked, "Are we having fun now?"

> "As water began entering Lock 7, our final lock of the day, all hell suddenly broke loose. The incoming water surged beneath our 600 SS boat."

I won't reveal the rest of the dialogue.

The next morning, Craig called to inform me what he had been told during the call to MAN. They felt the problem was a failed coolant pressure sensor. Craig proceeded to order a new sensor and drive belt, and had them overnighted to Ess-Kay. He promised he would return to Oswego as soon as the parts arrived, but he continued to insist that he wasn't able to get the proper filter for the generator.

How do I tell Elaine this? That thought flashed through my brain!

Craig arrived at noon and installed the sensor and belt. Another test run resulted in maximum rpm from both engines. While we waited for Craig to receive a certified warranty notification from MAN, I topped off the fuel tanks and pumped out the waste sewage tank.

Because Craig was unable to acquire the correct generator fuel filter, we would have no heat at the helm when traveling on the cold lake water. I kept repeating, "We will have heat for sleeping when we get to the Welland, I promise."

We collected the bedding we had brought and what Elaine found in the staterooms, so we could wrap them around ourselves at the helm as we huddled together driving the open boat. The water temperature remained at thirty-nine degrees as we departed on the three-hour run to the Welland Canal.

After traveling for fifteen miles, we encountered solid fog. Immediately afterwards, a weather bulletin reported a severe storm in the center of the lake with sixty-mile-per-hour winds. Our radar confirmed the approach of a severe storm. Turning around, we raced back to Oswego Marina.

After enduring another frosty night, we started our sixth day at six o'clock in the morning, pulling out from the marina and then cruising at forty miles per hour. A half-hour later, we were again enveloped in solid fog, with forty-degree water temperature. I slowed down to half speed.

Our planned three-hour trip now extended to a four-hour very cold ride.

We finally entered into Port Weller at ten-thirty in the morning. Tying off, I called to check in with Canadian Immigration and Customs for our passage through the Welland Canal. Dan, our trusted assistant, was once again ready to board the boat.

After waiting for an hour and a half, we were ordered to proceed to Lock 1, and instructed to follow the Tall Ship DENIS SULLIVAN into the Lock. A smaller boat was called to follow us.

In Lock 2, the DENIS SULLIVAN had a very difficult time staying on the wall. The entering water pushed the ship out into the center of the lock. Using their thrusters, the ship was driven back into the wall so hard I heard the hull's wooden planking snapping and breaking.

This wasn't a good omen.

Exiting from Lock 2, we were called to move to the forward position ahead of DENIS SULLIVAN in Locks 3, 4, 5, 6, and 7. We collectively agreed that this would make a faster trip through the Welland, since the DENIS SULLIVAN was slow to exit, and Dan knew Lock 8 wasn't in operation due to Lake Erie's low water.

As water began entering Lock 7, our final lock of the day, all hell suddenly broke loose. The incoming water surged beneath our 600

SS boat, thereby creating what I describe as a huge bubble or mountain of water. It immediately raised our twenty-five-ton vessel at least two feet or more straight up, and then caused the boat to tip violently to starboard and slide off the mountain of water.

Glancing forward, I couldn't see my wife. "Where's Elaine?" I yelled before I saw her lying on the bow of the boat with the safety rope still in her hand. Glancing aft to the rear, I didn't see Dan. Is he in the water? My brain was screaming!

Elaine stirred and looked at me. I hand-signaled her to cleat the safety line, which now caused the stern to swing off the bubble of water and slide toward the north wall.

I jumped down from the helm and ran the thirty feet to the stern. Dan was staggering as he tried to get up, and I snagged the safety line just before it slid into the water. "Thank you, Lord. He's not in the water!" flashed through my mind.

In the same motion, I managed to cleat the line to the port cleat. Using the safety line, I tried to pull the stern back toward the south wall, but to no avail. I quickly realized that the angle of the safety line to the south wall wouldn't stop the stern from hitting the north wall.

Dan was now on his feet, and he began pushing the stern off the north wall, which was seventy-six feet away from where we needed to be. We had to avoid hitting the wall, as the damage could possibly sink the boat. I raced back to the helm to use the propellers and thruster to assist Dan.

The stern of the 600 SS just touched the wall before we were able to recover control. We were immensely fortunate to suffer only a minor scratch instead of a destroyed and sinking yacht.

We were safe!

I called Welland Control. They heard some words perhaps not previously heard on the VHF. The incoming water had slowed, and we were now very slowly lifted the remaining forty feet. I demanded to make a formal report. I wasn't going to leave the lock until this was confirmed.

When we reached the top, no one was anywhere to be seen. I didn't move. The DENIS`SULLIVAN was impatiently sounding its air

*We shared our dangerous Welland Canal lock adventures with the Tall Ship DENIS SULLIVAN on this far-from-routine cruise.*

> "Despite the cold temperatures, stress, and sleepless nights, neither of us ended up with so much as a cold, just some very chilly early spring days in 2004 on the waters of the Great Lakes."

horn to make me exit the lock. Finally, Welland Control responded and defined where all three vessels could tie off in the canal so authorities could board and assess the damage.

The Seaway Welland captain boarded and said he had seen Elaine fall when he reviewed the video of what happened. He looked at her and asked, "Are you okay?"

"Yes," Elaine answered.

He reported that the third power craft in the group was a regular vessel passing through the Welland. "They agreed they had never experienced this level of turbulence. They hit the wall harder than ever before."

The captain reviewed our damage. In addition, he explained the emergency calls that I could have made at the instant of the problem. I, however, pointed out I wouldn't have had time to use the VHF to call.

I also pointed out this information was never made available in any form or place in our numerous travels through the canal. He agreed. I immediately recorded the communication rules and regulations, which I would use a number of times on subsequent trips through the Welland.

Dan stayed with us until we reached Marlon Marina. He retrieved his car and drove us to a fantastic restaurant, where the three of us relived the day and celebrated the fact we were alive and well. Dan was well paid that night—he had been so essential in saving the 600 SS from severe damage.

Back on board, finally warm because the heat pump was operating on the shore power, Elaine and I gave thanks to the Lord for keeping the yacht safe and for saving us from a terrible accident. We were truly blessed by His presence and protection.

The next day, with great relief, we docked the 600 SS at Marine Max Cleveland and were provided a chauffeured eighty-mile ride home.

A routine six-day trip turned into a most challenging eight-day cruise filled with wild experiences, increased knowledge, and the opportunity to expand our network of support companies and individuals who would assist us in so many ways during our future water adventures.

Upon our return home, we requested a personal meeting with Steve to air our frustrations and summarize the trip. He listened, thanked us, and commended us. "You both did a super job under very stressful conditions."

Despite the cold temperatures, stress, and sleepless nights, neither of us ended up with so much as a cold, just some very chilly early spring days in 2004 on the waters of the Great Lakes.

I had begun my personal journey to become an outstanding captain on the Great Lakes after purchasing our first Great Lakes pleasure craft in 1992. Neither Elaine nor I could have envisioned the learning experiences that we would face as we explored the Great Lakes and Inland Waters, confronting Mother Nature and God's creation, as we learned what it takes to be safe and survive on the water. ∎

# CHAPTER 15

# Managing Mud, Misery, and Rising Waters on a Luxury Meridian

**HOW CAN** a relatively straightforward assignment turn so quickly into a thirty-seven-day nightmare?

A question Elaine and I asked ourselves over the years.

We were given fifteen days in April to pilot a brand new million-dollar, thirty-five-ton yacht 1,700 miles from Minneapolis, Minnesota to Catawba Island, Ohio.

The nightmare began as soon as we entered the Mississippi River. The river was fifteen feet ABOVE flood stage, and continued to rise until the entire Upper Mississippi River was closed on the fourth day of our assignment.

Where could we find a safe place to store this new, very expensive yacht in the flooded and closed Upper Mississippi River?

That worry was the first of many dangerous situations and difficult questions we grappled with to safely complete the mission.

In early April of 2008, I received a call from the general manager of Marine Max Catawba, asking if I was available to meet with him. I was surprised, as the ice had just recently left Lake Erie, and only fishing boats were on the water. In fact, our Sea Ray wasn't scheduled to be splashed until May 1. The weather could still be stormy, and freezing temperatures were still possible, making it way too cold to get excited or even think about being out on the Great Lakes.

First, Tom summarized the plan for the coming annual Catawba Island Boat Show in Ohio, set for the weekend of May 3-5, 2008, at the Catawba Island Yacht Club. That was less than one month away.

The main attraction for the Marine Max floating presentation at the boat show was going to be a luxurious 2007 58 Pilot House Meridian Yacht built at the Meridian factory in Arlington, Washington. Current road load restrictions in Wisconsin, Indiana, Michigan, and Ohio didn't permit the thirty-five-ton vessel to be transported by truck in or through these states. But it had to arrive in time for the show.

First, Tom explained his plan now under consideration: to have it trucked to the Marine Max facility in Bayport, Minnesota, splashed into the St. Croix River, piloted down the Mississippi River to the Illinois River, then up into Lake Michigan and around to Catawba Island.

"You are the only captain I would trust to do this job," were his next words.

I recall just sitting there, probably with my mouth open, hesitating to even respond. I had to let this plan sink in.

"I have to make a decision today," Tom continued. "The Meridian factory is presently disassembling the boat in order to load it onto an east-bound trailer. It will have to be re-assembled wherever we splash it. Bayport Marine Max can handle that job."

He added, "I can't think of another option."

143

Long before boating season began on the Great Lakes, Elaine and I accepted an assignment to deliver a luxury yacht, the 2007 Piilot House Meridian, from Minnesota to Catawba Island.

I responded immediately. "I've kept the charts for the Mississippi and Illinois rivers ever since Elaine and I planned our (aborted) Big Loop winter cruise. I am confident we can do this, barring unknown or unplanned surprises." I added that I would only do this with Elaine as my first mate and with the ability to hire support if I believed I needed extra assistance.

"Let's do this!" Tom appeared pleased and relieved.

Upon arrival at home, I looked at Elaine in my normal way and before I could utter a word, she asked, "Well, what have you promised to do today? It'd better be in a warm place!"

"How about starting a trip in northern Minnesota within a week or two?"

I will only have you guess how she responded.

I explained the trip. Since it included a great stretch of our aborted "Great Loop" trip, I tried to convince her. "Just imagine how we'll enjoy the Mississippi on this brand-new luxury yacht, with all expenses paid! And we even get paid for our efforts."

Like the many challenges we faced on the water in the past sixteen years, I got a smile and a hug, and we started to plan.

On April 19, Marine Max Catawba received word the Meridian was reassembled and in the water in Bayport, Minnesota. We rented a car and loaded it with our personal items and my list of spare parts, fluids, filters, safety items (including a six-person inflatable raft), and numerous other items we might need.

At 5:30 a.m., on April 20, we departed from Catawba, Ohio for the seven-hundred-mile, eleven-hour drive to Bayport. Arriving at 3:30 in the afternoon, we immediately loaded our gear onto the Meridian.

Elaine and I met with the Bayport Marine Max manager, who informed us that Captain Duane and First Mate Mike would accompany us to Chicago, since the Mississippi and Illinois rivers were above flood stage. "Extra hands on board will help make this a safer trip."

He explained that they would fly from Chicago to New Orleans to pick up another boat and return it up the Mississippi to Bayport. "This timing will help both teams."

This Meridian vessel featured an upper area for the helm (the control center for the boat, called the pilot house), which was accessible both from the lower lounge and from the outer deck of the boat.

The Meridian is more than sixty feet long, with an extended swim platform. Its beam is almost eighteen feet wide, and she requires more than five feet of water. Based on the fact that the Mississippi was fifteen feet above flood and the Illinois was seven feet above flood, I didn't expect to have depth problems.

The Meridian was powered with twin Cummins diesels, each at seven hundred horsepower. Her total weight was approximately seventy thousand pounds (thirty-five tons) fully loaded, and she carried eight hundred gallons of diesel in a single tank.

Above the main center lounge and galley stretched an open upper deck with canvas cover and helm controls. A swing lift on the aft's upper deck would be used to load a dinghy onto the roof deck over the lounge.

The lower forward area included two large master staterooms, one with tub and shower, and the other with only a shower. The third stateroom was smaller, with two bunk beds and an adjoining head and shower. A washing machine and dishwasher provided comforts of home.

Before departure, I measured the Meridian's height as she rested in the water. I wanted to be certain her clearance dimension was indeed twenty feet, as described in the specifications. Overhead

*The scenery was spectacular for most of the voyage, but the flood waters made the journey highly dangerous, adding three weeks to what should have been a ten-day journey.*

*We had frequent concerns about the height of the Meridian because the Mississippi was expected to rise more than eighteen feet above flood.*

obstructions are measured from normal water levels, and with the flooding, I needed to keep track of how many feet above flood we were experiencing, so we would know if she could clear any overhead structures we might encounter.

At 6:30 p.m. the same day, the four of us departed Bayport, motoring directly into the St. Croix River. On that beautiful spring evening, we cruised the twenty-five miles down the river to enter the turbulent flooded Mississippi River. Once on the Mississippi, we instantly encountered the increased current, high water, and massive amounts of floating and underwater debris.

Passing through the Mississippi River's Lock 2 and 3, I was becoming familiar with how the Meridian responded with its twin Cummins diesels and bow thruster for handling the raging current.

After passing through Lock 3 at approximately eight o'clock that night, Captain Duane recommended we tie off for the night at Slippery's Marina in Wabasha, the only marina nearby. It was flooded, empty of any boats, and offered no electrical power, but we were able to find a safe spot to tie off.

Elaine and I expressed great relief when we moored the boat. We had driven seven hundred miles in eleven hours to Bayport, loaded our gear, and had completed another one hundred miles on the swollen Mississippi. A long day, but successful. So far.

No local businesses were open for dinner, so we ate on board and retired early.

On April 21, our second day, we were underway at 5:30 a.m. After untying and releasing the boat, First Mate Mike announced,

*Floating debris was a serious problem. The swift river currents swept everything from buoys to large appliances, furniture, big trees, and even small buildings past our bow.*

# "The flood waters were so high that most of the marinas normally selling fuel were totally flooded and, in some cases, totally covered with water."

"The water is three to five feet higher than last night." My immediate thought was that another three to five feet would put us at eighteen feet above flood. I then realized that the statement "feet above flood" didn't define how we would proceed on the river. The data we needed was "Are the locks open?"

Debris was everywhere: trees with their entire root systems were riding high in the water, along with washing machines, dryers, furniture, timbers, and countless household items all floating on the fast current. Some of the navigation cans marking the channel had broken free from their moorings and were floating on the fast-moving water. Those cans still attached to their moorings were being pushed under the water, and they popped up unexpectedly from their submerged graves. All four of us had to watch for floating debris and underwater deadheads.

While waiting for Lock 8, I calibrated and reset the autopilot (AutoHelm) that provided a compass heading on the chart plotter and its control display.

At that point, the generator quit. We immediately felt the cold temperatures of April on the Mississippi. I gave the helm to Captain Duane and climbed down into the engine compartment to check on the generator. I found the breaker tripped to "off." Resetting the breaker, I was relieved to hear the generator restart. It appeared to be okay. I assumed we had collected some debris that momentarily blocked the intake of river water, causing the generator to overheat.

The flood waters were so high that most of the marinas normally selling fuel were totally flooded and, in some cases, totally covered with water. Finally, after clearing Lock 11 in Dubuque, Iowa, we found a source for fuel, but we were only able to buy fifty gallons. Not only was the high water worrisome, but now we had to be constantly on the lookout for available fuel.

The Meridian's combined engines will burn forty to fifty gallons per hour at full throttle, but traveling with the river water, we were burning more like twenty to thirty gallons per hour. I estimated we were going to consume around three hundred gallons of diesel per day, and the 58 Pilot House Meridian diesel tank holds eight hundred gallons.

The "tows," as they are called on the inland rivers, consist of multiple barges tied together and pushed by a tugboat. The farther south we traveled, the more northbound tows we encountered. I assumed that the huge southbound current meant tows couldn't be controlled when moving with the current. I don't recall passing one.

When we saw a tow coming upriver in our direction, we often received a VHF call from the tow captain ordering "Slow down!" The wake produced by the Meridian was at times a couple of feet high. This wave of water could possibly push the lead barges to starboard, or toward the shore. Its effects could even be worse if the barges were empty. In addition, the freeboard on the gunwale of the tugboat pushing the barges sits very low in the water, so it wouldn't take a very large wake to wash over the tug. Looking down from the Meridian, I realized our wake would most likely flood their dining room.

The extra strong current of the flooded river would also carry our wake farther downstream, so upbound tugs warned us of their presence very early. Sometimes the communication would become quite tense, but we did our best to comply, as we had no wish to cause them problems. In fact, we could be charged if a tow was damaged due to our negligence.

We often met upbound tows with as many as fifteen barges tied together, three across and five rows in length, being pushed by a huge tug. The dimensions of a single tow with fifteen barges measure 1,000 feet long and 105 feet wide. Adding a fifty- or sixty-foot tug pushing this mass results in a gigantic tow, with a length of 1,200 feet, making a continuous unit almost one-quarter-mile long. Keep in mind that the Upper Mississippi locks are 1,200 feet long and 120 feet wide.

Each lock on the Mississippi raises or lowers the vessel an average of fifteen feet. When we were in the 1,200-foot lock, we wouldn't tie off to wait for the water to be released, since we could easily maneuver in the lock. In a few cases, we returned upstream and had to wait for the lock to be filled with vessels, in order to be lifted the approximately fifteen feet.

Exiting the Mississippi to enter the Illinois River equates to a total drop in elevation of 390 feet in our 450 miles of travel from the St. Croix River. This equates to about the same elevation change of 326 feet when passing through the seven locks in the twenty-three miles of the Welland Canal.

After passing through Lock 12, we made a decision to find a place to tie off for our second night. Captain Duane searched the paper charts and found Savanna City Marina, located on the east side of the river. "Let's be on the lookout for the marina. I'm hungry and I'm looking forward to a good dinner."

Just then, Elaine announced, "I see a dock down that channel," as she pointed to the port side.

I stopped the boat. We all looked to determine if we might tie-off there. As soon as I decided to enter the channel, I immediately noted the strong current carrying us down the channel, so I quickly turned the boat around to position the bow into the current.

A small marina floating dock used for tying off boats to obtain fuel was on the starboard side, but Captain Duane, who was at the stern, commented it wouldn't hold the boat. "I think we can wade to dry land," he commented. "So, I think we should move upstream, drop the anchor, and let the anchor rope out to let us move back."

I moved upstream, dropped the anchor, and made certain it was firmly holding the boat. Releasing the anchor line, I allowed the current to carry the boat slowly down the canal. When Captain Duane signaled to stop, we tied off the stern to the dock, then attached safety lines from the Meridian to poles holding the dock in place.

Removing our shoes and carrying them, we waded about fifty yards in six inches of water to reach dry land. We found an open restaurant three blocks away.

This method of using the anchor in the current was so simple, but I had never navigated in currents like we were experiencing. I specifically added this trick to my captain's memory bank.

We spent an enjoyable dinner getting to know each other and reviewing the second day. Captain Duane expressed his concern about the rising water. "We aren't yet halfway to the Illinois River. With the water continuing to rise, I'm worried about the river being closed because of water overflowing the locks."

We hoped for the best and returned to the Meridian.

Another early start on the third day, Tuesday, April 22, at 5:30 in the morning. Pulling out of the marina channel, we had to wait for the railroad bridge to open so we could pass through. The river had continued to rise overnight.

Clearing Lock 15 just south of Davenport, Iowa, we heard the VHF report: "Lock 17 is closed due to water overflowing the lock." When Captain Duane called Lock 17, the recorded message confirmed the news. He checked the river charts, but couldn't find any marinas between Locks 15 and 17.

At that instant, I became very afraid. As the assigned captain, I felt totally responsible for this new million-dollar boat. We were in the middle of the flooded and raging Mississippi River struggling to keep the boat safe, and now we needed to find a safe harbor. My assignment was to deliver this boat to the boat show. I envisioned total failure.

I remembered seeing two marinas in Bettendorf, so I turned the boat back upstream. We returned up through Lock 15 and approached the first small marina. From the helm, I looked down into its narrow entrance. To my complete surprise, the water of the marina was at least one-and-one-half feet lower than the river.

I called out, "The water is being sucked out of the marina! We have to find a marina that allows the water to run through it."

The next marina, in the center of Bettendorf, had a narrow entrance at the downriver end of a floating concrete walkway. The massive concrete structure continued upriver a good distance, and then angled to the very high river bank. It was solidly attached to the river walkway and was definitely designed for flooding like this. Because the river water was flowing under the walkway and through the marina, there was no danger of the water being sucked out.

The concrete barrier also forced the floating debris of trees and junk to pass by the marina. This marina would be safe, the perfect place to dock and wait for the water level to subside. This was where we needed to be. I shouted above the noise of the rushing water, "Now, if we can only stay here!"

We found an inside dock close to the river bank that appeared to be the most protected location, and we tied off, happy to find an electrical power station located at our position. I connected the Meridian's electrical cable to the power station, but found there wasn't any 50-amp electricity. Checking the marina, we didn't find anyone to assist us, but a set of stairs led up the river bank into a covered walkway.

Elaine and I climbed the stairs and found the walkway ended at the Isle of Capri Casino and Hotel, where we inquired about dockage at the marina. We were directed to the gift shop. There, the manager told us we were welcome to stay at the marina until the river opened. Electrical power was ten dollars per day, and the marina also had security cameras with additional walk-through by security personnel.

I turned to Elaine. "The Lord just answered my prayer."

I paid for three days of electrical power, and when we returned to the boat, the power was already on. What a blessing to have security, power, and a safe place in the flood. We stopped for a moment and again thanked the Lord.

That evening the four of us enjoyed a delicious dinner at the casino, and Elaine and I even left some money in the slot machines.

The next day, Wednesday, April 23, was only our fourth day on the mighty Mississippi. Using my computer, I checked on the latest update of Lock 17. It indicated that the earliest forecast was for the lock to open Friday evening, or Saturday, contingent on the rainfall in the Upper Mississippi Valley. The river still hadn't crested at the predicted level of eighteen and one-half feet. It was currently sixteen feet above flood.

After considering this data, Captain Duane announced that he and First Mate Mike had decided to rent a car and drive back to Minnesota to wait out the situation there. They still had to bring the boat up the Mississippi from New Orleans to Bayport.

I called Tom at Catawba Marine Max and summarized the situation, confirming the bad news that the boat was not going to arrive in time for the Catawba Boat Show. Disappointed, he expressed his relief to hear the Meridian was in a safe place at least, and that we were okay. He recommended we return home, but I wanted to stay another day or two to thoroughly check all fluid levels, as I hadn't had the opportunity in Bayport before departure. I also wanted to top off the fuel if it was available here.

I estimated we only had 250 gallons remaining, and we were only about halfway to the Illinois River. Including the twenty-five gallons we added on the second day, we had consumed about six hundred gallons traveling to Bettendorf.

Elaine and I walked to the casino and inquired about fuel. They said they had 1,500 gallons to sell, so with a feeling of great relief, we

# "At that moment, I became very afraid…We were in the middle of the flooded and raging Mississippi, struggling to keep the boat safe."

topped off our fuel tank and emptied our sewage holding tank. We were ready to continue on our way as soon as the river opened.

I took the available time to check all the fluid levels. When forced to start out in a hurry with a brand-new boat, captains must rely on the preparation team to have checked and filled all the fluid reservoirs. In our rush to get underway, I didn't personally check any oil or coolant levels, since Captain Duane said he and the technicians had checked everything.

Another lesson learned! Those checks may have been made, but I concluded fluids had not been added. I used one gallon of engine oil, two gallons of battery water, one gallon of transmission oil, and had to top off the trim tabs reservoir and thruster gear boxes.

I then realized Captain Duane took his fenders, also called bumpers, when the two men departed. We had used them, in addition to mine, to avoid damage to the Meridian. I needed replacements to ensure the boat's safety before leaving the marina.

I called a marine supply store, located about three miles away, to order all the various oils, distilled water, and bumpers I would need. They agreed to deliver all of my order to the marina the next day, Saturday, April 26.

I continued to check the status of Lock 17. The projections were now indicating a possibility of opening the river midweek, around April 30. I kept Tom updated as to our status, and with this latest forecast, he said, "Come home."

The casino manager agreed to keep the Meridian there until the locks opened. They would charge for dockage and electricity, ten dollars per weekday and twenty dollars per day for Friday, Saturday, and Sunday. I paid for our stay.

On Saturday, April 26, the materials ordered from the marine supply store arrived in the early morning. After loading and securing the new supplies, Elaine and I closed up the Meridian and took the casino shuttle to the airport. There we rented a car and drove home.

I continued to monitor the water status at Lock 17. Finally, nineteen days later, on May 15, I saw a projected opening of Lock 17: May 17.

## WE FINALLY RESUME THE ODYSSEY

During the three weeks of waiting, I had been diligently searching for a captain to join Elaine and me in bringing the Meridian home. I finally made contact with a young captain named John, who said he had some experience working on the Eastern Intercostal Waterway. He was at home in Sandusky, Ohio, and was available for the estimated eight or ten days necessary to bring the Meridian to Catawba. I interviewed him and decided he would be helpful to assist me at the helm on the ten-to-fourteen-hour days we anticipated. I arranged for Tom to interview him, to be certain he was agreeable to my recommendation. Tom agreed.

I kept John up to date and immediately called him when I learned the Upper Mississippi was opened. The water levels were

*Among our many challenges was finding safe marina accommodations for the Meridian when river levels were close to eighteen feet above normal.*

still at fifteen feet above flood, so the locks would be full, but open. No rain was in the forecast. I also verified that the Illinois River was still at eight feet above flood, but at least it was passable.

John agreed we would leave the next morning. I rented a car and the three of us departed for Bettendorf on May 16. Upon arrival, we made a thorough check of the Meridian while I oriented John about the features of the vessel. I concluded the vessel was as we left it, returned the car, and paid the casino the charges agreed upon.

At about six o'clock that night, I made a computer check on Lock 17. It was still open with the same water level, 17.9 feet above flood, and with the same conditional statement: if the water rose to 18.1 feet, Lock 17 would again be closed. I decided we would take the chance and depart at six o'clock the following morning.

All of us walked the breakwater to examine the Mississippi. It appeared to me to be the same as three weeks ago: a raging flow of water filled with debris. John seemed surprised to see and hear what he had agreed to do.

Engine start was as planned, and we entered the fast-moving Mississippi very early that morning. When I called Lock 15, we were advised they would be ready for us to enter. The three of us were on constant watch, directing our path through the debris. Calling ahead, we verified that Locks 16 and 17 were open and waiting for our arrival. We made it through without incident.

After clearing Lock 17, I started searching for a place to stay that night. After a number of unsuccessful phone calls, I finally made contact with the Pier Restaurant and Barge Dock in Quincy, Illinois.

# "Elaine grabbed and hugged me so hard, it took me a few minutes to catch my breath."

The owner told me he had a fixed barge in the Mississippi with a restaurant adjacent to the barge. "You can tie off for the night on the barge, and the restaurant will be open. Call when you're close, and I'll help you get from the barge to the restaurant."

Arriving at the barge, we found the current at least eight to ten knots—which was faster than any area on the trip so far. We used multiple lines to make certain the Meridian would only move with the barge if it were to break free from its multiple moorings.

The owner came and helped us climb over numerous railings and docks to finally reach the restaurant. After another grueling twelve-hour day, we enjoyed a marvelous dinner and a glass of wine.

The next morning, engine start was at 6:15. We all worked together to untie and clear the Meridian from the barge in the fast current. When I called Lock 21, we were informed we had fifteen minutes to reach the lock or we would have to wait for a large tow to pass through.

I pushed the Meridian hard to reach the lock on time, while still avoiding the debris, and we successfully made it. Once in the lock, I told the new captain, "The helm is yours."

The current through the lock was very strong and might have been increasing as we were being lowered. In a loud voice, I pointed out, "John we've moved too close to the lock gate. Move us back! We have a 105-foot-wide tow in front of the lock doors."

No response.

"Move us back!" I yelled.

Nothing happened!

I was shocked to see through the partially open lock doors that the tow was located right up next to the lock opening. The 105-foot-wide tow was evidently empty, and I wondered how we were going to pass it.

Six guys holding poles used to pass lines were standing on the very front of the high barges, about the same height as the Meridian helm. We all knew they would never be able to prevent a change in the direction of our thirty-five-ton Meridian.

In that instant, I also realized the river water was passing under the barges rather than being diverted to the port side of the Meridian. The water flow was going to carry us directly into the tow!

The doors were almost open when the lockmaster shouted over the VHF, "Turn hard to port right after the second pillar. You don't have much room."

Our captain still appeared frozen, so I yelled, "I'm taking the helm" as I pushed him aside. I immediately turned the Meridian to port. In the same instant, the current catapulted us forward, directly at the tow. Realizing we didn't have any of the normal water flow to assist us in making the turn, I would have to make the turn under full power.

My eyes focused on that second pillar as we were thrown forward with the ten-mile-per-hour current. With all my instincts, experience, and "what ifs," I concentrated on the port bow just clearing the second pillar, and then I quickly turned the rudder hard to port and simultaneously slammed the starboard and then the port into gear, with the throttles full forward. Maybe I closed my eyes for a second, but we were clear.

*Among our many challenges was finding safe marina dockage for the Meridian when water levels were so elevated and many marinas were completely flooded.*

As I glanced over and back at the tow, I saw those six men celebrating, pumping the air with their fists. I'm sure they felt as relieved as I did.

Elaine grabbed and hugged me so hard, it took me a few minutes to catch my breath. John might have been angry, but I didn't care. I knew in my heart that he wouldn't have reacted fast enough.

We had a very quiet ride to Lock 22, with me at the helm. I then gave him the helm to pass through Locks 23 and 24.

After Lock 25, we found ourselves at the entrance to the Illinois River and the town of Grafton. When I called Grafton Marina, I learned they didn't have fuel, but they did have open docks and an entrance deep enough for us. We told them we would be back for the night, but we definitely needed to find fuel.

The next marina, Piasa Marina, had fuel, but as we began our entrance, we saw silted sand stretched across the entrance and called to tell the marina that would prevent us from entering. They suggested Alton Marina, so we cruised another five miles downriver.

"Well, what do we have here?" I called to Elaine as we passed by the entrance in order to enter upstream into the marina. Tipped on its port side and grounded was a 42 Sea Ray Sundancer with a jet ski on the swim platform. Turning to Elaine, I said, "It looks like the Sea Ray that Captain Duane and First Mate Mike were going to bring up from New Orleans. What a coincidence, if it is."

The marina harbormaster had seen us and called with instructions. "There is serious shoaling on the starboard side of the entrance, and the current is very strong. You'll have stay to port and power in. Be careful entering, as there's not much room."

Seeing the grounded boat, I was determined to stay outboard and come in at an angle. We placed lines on the stern, bow, and mid-ship, ready to be thrown if needed. John was to shout out depth as we approached the entrance, and Elaine was stationed on the bow with lines cleated. When she put her lifejacket on, I tied a line around her before she went to the bow, and held onto the line through the pilot house starboard door opening, in case we were suddenly stopped by the shoaling and she fell.

Concentrating on the approach, I maintained plenty of power. As we approached the entrance, the depth call-outs sounded good. We entered the marina fast. Once there, I threw the props into a hard reverse, and we successfully stopped, safe in the marina.

At the fuel dock we were met by Captain Duane and First Mate Mike. As we began to fuel, Captain Duane begged, "Pat, would you pull me off the sand bar?"

I shook my head, "Duane, you know this is a new boat, unfit for anything like that. We don't have lines heavy enough, the cleats are only for holding it to a mooring, and the current is too strong to even hold a position while attempting to line up to pull your boat.

"I'm very sorry, Duane, but I won't even try. You need to call a towboat, as I am certain that sand has silted around the bottom. Only a towboat will be able to rock it free."

Duane turned and slowly walked away. A sad moment, as we both knew I couldn't help. I was quick to pay for the fuel and return to Grafton for the night.

The entrance into the Grafton Marina was a duplicate of what I did in Alton. We found a dock where the bow could face into the nine-mile-per-hour current flowing through the marina.

Another twelve-hour day.

At 6:15 on the morning of May 19, we departed Grafton and headed up the Illinois River. The current was as fast as the Mississippi's had been, but in this case, we were going upstream, which would require using twice as much fuel. This final river leg of our trip to reach Lake Michigan was approximately 350 miles. We would be consuming about forty gallons per hour—a lot of diesel, so we needed to fuel whenever it was available.

There is a succession of eight locks on the Illinois River, the Des Plaines River, and the Chicago Sanitary Canal. Approaching our first lock on the Illinois River, the La Grange Lock and Dam, I called the lock master and requested information. His reply? "La Grange Lock is closed. Proceed over the dam."

My quick and immediate response was, "What do you mean, proceed over the dam? I draw five feet, and I need another foot to be safe."

"Captain, our dams are hydraulically operated," he explained. "In high water like this, we lower the dam so it's flat to the bottom of the river. You may only feel a slight bump going over because of the change in water flow, but you'll have more than eight feet of water."

Totally surprised, I didn't respond.

I slowed down to carefully cross the area where I determined the dam would have been. Safely over the first one, I gave a very big sigh of relief. The same procedure was done for Lock 7, Peoria Lock and Dam.

I called ahead to Henry's Harbor Marina in Henry, Illinois, and was told dockage was available, but their fuel was limited to three hundred gallons. I requested it be saved for our arrival. He took advantage of us, charging five dollars per gallon, when normally we had paid under two dollars per gallon, but I was thankful to have the fuel.

Due to the extremely high water, we had to tie off on an ancient rock lock wall. Fortunately, we had sufficient electrical cable to plug into electric service, and all our fenders were used to protect the Meridian from the rocks. After a wonderful meal at Henry's Harbor Marina, we retired early, exhausted after fourteen hours of travel.

*Elaine and I breathed huge sighs of relief when we passed through the Chicago Sanitary and Ship Canal and headed onto Lake Michigan.*

May 20: Engines on at 6:15 a.m., and we were underway. The current was much slower now, and we were relieved to be under less stress. We passed through two locks, but we were stopped at Lock 3, Brandon Lock and Dam. We couldn't tie off as we waited in the current for the passing of two tow units. Finally, we successfully passed through and entered the Des Plaines River in the city of Joliet. We found an open spot with shore power on the river's Joliet Park Wall.

We tied off after a thirteen-hour day.

All three of us were totally exhausted. John said he would take a walk and bring back some food. Elaine and I opened a bottle of wine and went topside to enjoy the view of Joliet as the sun slowly dipped below the horizon. Sleep was welcome that night.

May 21: engines on at 6:00 a.m., and we were underway on the Des Plaines River, heading to the Chicago Sanitary and Ship Canal. Because we were low on fuel and wanted to have a full tank entering Lake Michigan, we left the canal and were able to find fuel. After topping off the tank, we re-entered the Sanitary and Ship Canal and proceeded through downtown Chicago, then exited out into Lake Michigan.

The Lake Michigan forecast called for north winds for the next few days. We needed to cross Lake Michigan the following day, and I wanted to be quartering the south-bound waves. The obvious solution was to head north for 120 miles to Port Washington, Wisconsin. Port Washington was our favorite port on the west coast of Lake Michigan south of Door County. We planned to stay there for the night.

I called the Port Washington harbormaster. Julie, our favorite gal, answered the phone and asked, "What in the world are you and Elaine doing on Lake Michigan so early in the year?" After updating her, we were assigned the end of Dock 4 with 50-amp service. Since our arrival would be after the marina closed, I provided credit card information and Julie agreed to place the receipt and gate key in the 50-amp electrical box.

We were all set for the beginning of the Great Lakes chapter of this adventure.

> "This experience on the Mississippi and Illinois Rivers increased my knowledge and confidence to be the best captain on fresh water."

Fortunately, this final leg of the delivery was uneventful. We made overnight stops at Cheboygan County Marina on May 22 and Port Huron Riverside City Marina on May 23.

At noon on May 24, we tied off the Meridian. Three weeks after our anticipated due date, the million-dollar yacht was safely delivered to Marine Max Catawba. Miraculously, we managed the entire adventure with only one minor surface scratch on the swim platform.

This 1,700-mile adventure on the St. Croix River, Mississippi River Waterway, Illinois River Waterway, Lake Michigan, Lake Huron, Lake St. Clair, and Lake Erie was a challenge that tested and further educated me as a captain.

Ten days of travel on the water was the actual time required to move the boat from Bayfield to Catawba Island, but the flooded Mississippi caused more than three weeks' delay for the delivery of the 58 PH Meridian.

This experience on the Mississippi and Illinois Rivers increased my knowledge and confidence to be the best captain on fresh water. But it was a wild adventure. ∎

*Fueled up and ready to go, the nine boats in our first Getaway awaited the start of the first long-range, extended voyage Elaine and I led to scenic spots throughout the Great Lakes.*

CHAPTER 16

# Pleasures and Perils During Group Getaways

**"SEA RAY I, SEA RAY I,** this is GOOD KARMA."

The VHF startled me when we were crossing Lake Ontario from Port Dalhousie to Toronto Harbor Front Marina.

"GOOD KARMA, SEA RAY 1 here. What's the problem?"

"SEA RAY I, GOOD KARMA." A very excited voice exclaimed, "The starboard engine alarm is on, and I don't know what to do! I don't want to shut off the starboard engine. I've never driven the boat with only one engine. What should I do?"

I needed to calm the caller and make certain GOOD KARMA would safely arrive in Toronto.

"GOOD KARMA, SEA RAY 1. Place the starboard in neutral and leave the starboard engine running, so cooling water will continue to be pumped through the engine and transmission. Use the port engine and transmission to keep the bow into the waves. I see you, and I am heading over to help. Don't worry!"

### GETAWAY PLANNING

Marine Max of Ohio was always searching for ways to expand their boat sales. From 1995 to 2010, I was a contract captain, called to deliver large pleasure craft and teach the Spouse-on-the-Water classes. My growing reputation generated inquiries from customers and sales personnel, asking Marine Max to arrange extended getaways that Elaine and I would lead. We had supervised some day cruises, but we were getting requests for long-range cruises lasting between one and two weeks.

Very few of the thousands of boats in the western basin of Lake Erie ever leave the lake, but many stories are told of those boats that ventured beyond Lake Erie. Not all tales are tragedies, but many tell of fearful times when boats hit submerged rocks and shoals, when they didn't know where to stay, and when they encountered severe storms and subsequently panicked.

Elaine and I planned "The Getaway" with Marine Max as a ten-to-fourteen-day cruise, where owners journeyed on their own boats within a group Elaine and I led. Cruising with other boats offered some confidence to boat owners who would normally hesitate to venture out on their own.

First I identified harbor locations willing to accept a group of ten boats, since the number of marinas capable or willing to accommodate a large group was limited. The availability of fuel, nearby dining facilities, sightseeing, and boat service facilities were then considered. Often the boaters had their own preferences of where to stay.

The preparations for the Getaway were extensive, and Elaine and I spent a lot of time working with the staff at Marine Max during the process. I needed to know each boat's cruising speed, what fuel was needed (gas or diesel), and the boat's physical size so I could determine necessary dock space. Most importantly, I needed to know whether the boat been properly maintained.

Marine Max agreed to make the overnight reservations and plan a few dinners. I would do an analysis of the boats' ages and maintenance histories. If maintenance care wasn't done by Marine Max, I requested the information from the owner. If at all possible, we wanted to avoid equipment failures that could interfere with the cruise. All participants understood they were responsible for their own equipment.

I also spent time, individually and in group meetings, with the boaters, to review safety issues, documentation requirements, and suggest what to bring or not to bring. Canadian Customs will not permit alcohol on board, and drug inspections are always a possibility. Boat registration and passports or the equivalent for everyone are also necessary. No firearms allowed.

This cruise to Toronto was our first planned Getaway cruise. Later, we would lead two other Getaways from Marine Max of Ohio: seven boats to Bay Harbor on Lake Michigan, and eleven boats on the St. Lawerence River, which included circumnavigating Lake Ontario. The Getaways all had challenging issues, but nothing like this first one in 2005.

### GETAWAY TO TORONTO, ONTARIO
July 13-22, 2005: 10 days

SEA RAY 1 (the name we used on the Getaway) was a new million-dollar 2005 Sea Ray 500DA. On board were three of us: Scott, a Marine Max experienced boater and salesman, Elaine, and me. On July 13, 2004, we departed from Marine Max on Lake Erie with four Sea Rays of various sizes and vintages following behind us. I don't recall the brands of the other boats, but they were all capable of running at the same speed.

On the way, we were joined by two boats off Kelleys Island, one off Vermilion, and a Sea Ray off Cleveland.

The ninth boat, a Sea Ray 510 from Toledo, had trouble starting and planned to catch up with us in Erie or Port Colborne. But, on its overnight stop on Lake Erie, a passenger fell on the swim platform, broke a leg, and was rushed to a hospital. Their trip was cancelled.

Was this a sign of more forthcoming challenges?

The original tenth boat, which hailed from Buffalo, New York, now became the ninth boat. It would join us at Port Colborne and pass through the Welland Canal with us.

A total of thirty-five people were on board the nine boats. Family members, couples, and other boat owners were taking advantage of the opportunity to expand their on-the-water experiences.

### FIRST NIGHT IN ERIE PENNSYLVANIA

Our first day consisted of a 130-mile trip, the longest leg of this Getaway. We had reservations at Bay Harbor Marina in Erie, which would accept our eight boats and provide sufficient gas and diesel fuel for the group.

When our boats safely arrived in Erie, we all fueled and enjoyed a potluck dinner on a beautiful summer evening. We reviewed the next day's plan: a sixty-mile cruise to Port Colbourne, Ontario,

> "Each of the eight boats was assigned to a specific position within the lock—wall or outside—and this determined their single-file position through the canal."

*Elaine and I led three Getaways on the SEA RAY I. All had challenges, but none like our first Getaway on the new million-dollar 2005 Sea Ray 500DA.*

PLEASURES AND PERILS DURING GROUP GETAWAYS

*The interior of the million-dollar 2005 Sea Ray 500D was elegant and well appointed.*

where we had reservations for all nine boats at Marlon Marine. The forecast was for seas at one to two feet, a perfect day for boating on Lake Erie.

## PORT COLBORNE, ONTARIO

Everyone arrived without incident in Port Colborne and called Canadian Customs and Immigration on their special phone. No one from Immigration came to perform a detailed inspection, and I was relieved.

I checked with each boat to make sure they fueled, so they would be ready for passing through the Welland Canal, then proceeding to overnight in Port Dalhousie before undertaking the thirty-mile cruise to Toronto.

The boat from Buffalo had arrived, so all were accounted for. We all gathered for dinner and instructions at the yacht club next door to Marlon Marine. I again explained the process for traveling through the twenty-three-mile-long Welland Canal. Everyone understood that seven locks would lower us 326 feet to Lake Ontario.

I had determined the placement of the boats based on length. Four pairs of boats with SEA RAY 1, the single, at the rear. Our Sea Ray 1, the ninth boat, would be last, since I wanted to be able to assist anyone who might run into trouble.

Each of the eight boats was assigned to a specific position within the lock—wall or outside—and this determined their single-file position through the canal. The first boat entering a lock was to go to the starboard wall, and the second boat would tie off on the first boat's port side. Of the pair, the wall boat always exited first, and then the outside boat.

I verified that each of the wall-assigned vessels had two adults capable of handling the Welland lines and a third adult at the helm. I also assigned three people to be on the outside boat, on the bow, helm, and swim platform, ready to assist the boat on the wall if assistance was required.

It was necessary to have people move to different vessels in order to meet this requirement. The realignment of people was to take place before we departed from Marlon Marine, since it wouldn't be possible once we were in the canal.

I also reviewed the process of entering the canal in the morning. Each boat had to register and pay its fee before we would be permitted to move through the canal. The order of boats through the canal was verified one more time, and I answered questions, addressed fears, and offered additional instructions.

That night, I was having difficulty falling asleep, but Elaine reassured me, "Hon, don't worry! I was watching the captains, and they all appeared to be ready. You've done a great job preparing them. Now, get some rest."

She was right. The next day we passed through the Welland smoothly and enjoyed the few miles on Lake Ontario from Port Weller to Port Dalhousie Marina. At the evening meeting, I prepared everyone for the cruise to Toronto. Everyone was pleased to explore Lake Ontario.

The next day, we were about thirty miles from Toronto, with seas between two and three feet and a northeast wind on the bow, when the urgent VHF message from GOOD KARMA startled us.

As we changed course and drove over toward GOOD KARMA, I told Scott and Elaine my plan. "I'm going to jump from our swim platform to GOOD KARMA's swim platform. It's the only way possible to get on board. These waves will do serious damage to both boats if we attempted to tie them together."

"You're crazy to do this!" Elaine protested.

"Hon, I've done this before. Please don't worry."

While cruising over to GOOD KARMA, I called all the boats and told them that C DRAGNET, with the most experienced captain and first mate, was now the lead boat, and all should follow them to Toronto. I informed them that GOOD KARMA only had one engine and I would be bringing the boat to Toronto. They were to prepare sufficient room on a dock and be ready to assist when we arrived.

I instructed Scott on my plan. We had to operate with precision, as two twenty-ton boats could be no closer than three feet apart in these rough seas. I explained that I would back up our boat to the

# "Everything I have done, as far back as I can remember, was approached with one goal: *Excel.*"

GOOD KARMA's swim platform. Once I got as close as possible, I would leave the helm, race to our swim platform, and jump to GOOD KARMA. Scott agreed to the plan.

"When I leave the helm, you must instantly take over and hold SEA RAY 1 in position. But be ready to pull away as soon as I jump." I continued, "If I fall in, I don't want to be a bumper between the boats."

Elaine was to stand on the swim platform with her arms up in the air to indicate the gap of space between the two swim platforms so I could make an accurate jump. She had the life ring to throw to me if, for some reason, I wasn't successful. I really didn't want to think about that.

"Elaine, as soon as I jump, yell 'STOP' to GOOD KARMA."

On the VHF, I called, "GOOD KARMA, SEA RAY 1. I'm right behind you. Using the your port engine, try to keep the bow directly into the waves without going forward. Try to keep the stern from swinging back and forth while I'm backing SEA RAY 1, so our swim platforms are facing each other. I'll be jumping onto your swim platform. When Elaine yells 'STOP,' put your port engine in neutral. Up until then, do your best to keep the boat as steady as possible, and don't make any quick moves. Do you understand?"

"SEA RAY 1, I'm ready."

With a nod from Scott and Elaine, I backed SEA RAY 1 to GOOD KARMA. Elaine signaled the distance I had to jump. I had to make two attempts because a wave changed the timing, so Elaine waved me off. Finally, her arms went straight up. I ran and safely jumped to GOOD KARMA.

My jump from swim platform to platform went as I had planned. I was so thankful that I didn't have to taste Lake Ontario's water.

I yelled to the captain, "Great job! Put the port in gear and hold the position." Previously I had requested he put the engine in neutral, so the port prop wouldn't be turning if I fell into the lake.

I quickly entered the engine compartment to inspect the starboard engine. The alarm was still sounding. No smoke or burning odor. The running engine wasn't hot, but the transmission was hot. I went topside and saw water exiting with the exhaust. Later, I decided to shut the starboard engine off when I felt the transmission had cooled.

The ride to Toronto was slow but uneventful. Once inside the city harbor, the captains assisted me in docking. Scott had already informed the harbormaster of the situation, and a Sea Ray technician was on his way.

Unfortunately, in our three-day stay in Toronto, the Sea Ray technician couldn't correct the problem. The owner arranged to have the boat taken to the nearest Sea Ray dealer, and the family returned to Ohio by car.

Elaine and I were grateful that our return to Port Dalhousie Marina, up the Welland, and into Port Colborne proceeded without any additional adventures.

However, a very serious life-threatening situation did develop on the Getaway cruise to Port Stanley, Ontario, which is located on the north shore of Lake Erie.

As we departed from Port Colborne on the tenth day, the sea was very rough, with west winds creating four-to-six-foot waves

*A very serious, life-threatening situation developed on our Getaway cruise to Port Stanley, Ontario, on Lake Erie's north shore.*

# "Being the best captain on the Great Lakes wasn't just a dream, it was what I expected of myself."

directly on the bow. The boats were running at an average of ten knots, or about twelve miles per hour. After three hours, the wind began to subside and we were able to increase our speed.

I suddenly noticed that one of the Getaway boats in front of us had installed their side canvas for protection from the wind and sea spray. The aft was entirely open.

The couple had two children, one about five and the other seven, but I didn't see the children in the boat. My intuition urged me to check on them, so I sped up to reach them. As we came alongside, I saw they didn't have their front windshield glass open.

I immediately called them on VHF. "I don't see your windshield glass open for incoming air, and your aft is open. You could be sucking in exhaust. Where are the kids?"

I saw the front window immediately open, but more importantly, I saw the mother, who had apparently been lying down on the helm bench, jump up and go below. The children were suddenly topside.

That afternoon, as soon as we docked at Kettle Creek in Port Stanley, Ontario, the mother came running up and wrapped her arms around me. Crying and holding me, she sobbed, "You saved our children! I was almost asleep when you called. When I went below, they were almost unconscious lying on the bed, and they were sick. Your call saved them."

I immediately asked to see the children, who appeared fine, but I asked the parents, "Should we have them checked out by an EMT? I'll call now." They didn't think that was necessary.

As she returned to their boat, the mother continued crying. She told everyone that I had saved her children. My thought was, "Thank the Lord!"

I know, to this very day, that the Lord, not I, was leading that afternoon. My efforts to become the best captain on the Great Lakes had just been validated. Even if I was the only one to know it.

Everything I have done, as far back as I can remember, was approached with one goal: *Excel*. Being the best captain on the Great Lakes wasn't just a dream, it was what I expected of myself, studied for, simulated, practiced, and prayed for. I didn't care what anyone else thought. I sought to learn, experience, and anticipate every situation at all times.

I obtained knowledge by reading, studying, and actually going on a boat and doing what I had studied. The final test for any challenge is to do what you prepare for. These chapters represent the actual execution of what was expected at the time of need.

I know it would be impossible to determine who is the best in a profession such as a captain of vessels. But the continued efforts to be educated and experienced in as many ways as humanly possible would make me a better captain—and a better person. After all, the lives of my wife, family, and all those I met on the water relied on me. I will never give up my *Anticipate* attitude. I am always ready. ■

*I know, to this very day, that the Lord, not I, was leading our Getaways.*

PLEASURES AND PERILS DURING GROUP GETAWAYS

# After Words

**WHEN I WAS SEVEN YEARS OLD,** the Mysterious Lake Superior took ahold of me, pulled me under Her cold and beautiful blue waters, and then released me to live another day. I have always believed it was a miracle that I lived, and I've believed that was because She wanted to claim my attention and imagination. I have never lost my fascination with Big Waters.

But with a handful of exceptions, my on-the-water adventures had to wait until I met the love of my life, Elaine Killey. Together, we were willing to step out of our comfort zone to become freshwater islanders and explorers of the Great Lakes and ocean waters. As soon as we purchased our first boat, I was determined to become the best and most experienced Captain possible. And Elaine became the best First Mate any Captain could want.

When I'm asked what drew me to boating, I will always say it was a fascination with the technology and precision of operating a vessel. But my answer is more complex than that. I was drawn to the history, geography, and natural wonders that reveal themselves to boaters. Captains learn something new every day, and Captains are constantly tested. I've lived my whole life facing challenges with a determination to be the best. Boating offers physical and intellectual challenges, as well as a new personal quest with limitless horizons.

As children, Elaine and I both endured great tragedies and difficulties, and I now believe that is the reason why we were always ready to attempt new adventures and challenging assignments. But in 2010, we knew it was time to sell our fourth ELEANA. In the aftermath of the 2008-10 recession, few large boats were being purchased, fuel prices had sharply increased, and transport services were declining. And we had other paths to explore.

My wife of sixty-two years and the mother of our three children is now with the Lord. I sorely wish Elaine could have been whispering in my ear as I wrote, so I could include her words and memories of our nautical escapades. But no adventure was undertaken or completed without her love, encouragement, laughter, tears, and constant support.

# Biography

**EXCEL! BE THE BEST!**

Those themes echo throughout Pat Winton's life.

At a very young age, he was baptized by Lake Superior and developed a life-long passion for Big Waters. Despite spending much of his childhood shuttled from one relative to another in a hardscrabble Finnish community, he completed high school with honors in 1957, and earned scholarships to, and a degree from, General Motors Institute (now Kettering University).

Winton's early career focused on the auto industry while he and his wife Elaine raised three children. He earned a master's degree in mechanical engineering from Wayne State University in Detroit, Michigan, and eventually became co-owner of an international company manufacturing automated machines for producing small electric motors. During those years, he wrote and published technical papers and patents.

As soon as they could, the Wintons built a cottage on an island, and their boating career began. Years later, after selling their island property, they realized they wanted to pursue a water-bound life full of adventures and challenges. They set a new career goal: to explore all of the Great Lakes and as many inland and ocean waterways as possible. To do this, they had to become a highly accomplished captain and first mate.

Winton transformed a boating hobby into their second career. After earning his United States Coast Guard Captain's License, he and Elaine led long-distance group boating getaways, evaluated yachts in production, and moved new yachts long distances, throughout the Great Lakes, Mississippi River, and both the Pacific and Atlantic oceans, often under extremely adverse conditions.

When Elaine's health began failing, Pat launched his third career at the age of 82: creative writing. His riveting coming-of-age memoir, *Farmed out in Ontonagon County*, chronicles his difficult youth in Michigan's Upper Peninsula. *Chasing Waves* is his second book.

www.ingramcontent.com/pod-product-compliance
Lightning Source LLC
Chambersburg PA
CBHW041554030426
42337CB00004B/50